"I'm so thrilled that this book exists. The Enneagram has absolutely changed my understanding of how to love the people in my life, deepened the quality of my marriage, and given me a vision for the person God designed me to be. This book makes the Enneagram easy to understand, with helpful stories, humor, warmth, and clear language. I'll need a case, at least."

Shauna Niequist, author of *Savor* and *Bread and Wine*

"What would you give to crack the biggest mystery in the world: Yourself? Why do we act, think, feel, and believe the way we do? I know of no better tool than the Enneagram. And I know of no better teachers of this tool than my friends Ian Cron and Suzanne Stabile. I use the Enneagram in my business and personal life every day. *The Road Back to You* will open your eyes to the depths of your heart."

Michael Hyatt, coauthor of *Living Forward*

"With *The Road Back to You*, the small number of books I recommend to absolutely everyone has increased by one. You couldn't ask for a better introduction to the Enneagram than what's found in this book and you couldn't ask for better guides than Cron and Stabile. If a modicum of self-awareness is needed to navigate life these days, let this book be your map."

Nadia Bolz-Weber, author of *Accidental Saints*

"Armed with delightful but incisive wit, Cron and Stabile help us explore our inner life by making the mystery of the Enneagram accessible. If you want to better understand yourself and those in the world around you, this insightful and brilliant book is a perfect place to begin."

Wm. Paul Young, author of *The Shack*

"The Enneagram has been a vital tool in my own personal journey of self-discovery, and *The Road Back to You* does a great job of making this ancient tool accessible for the modern Christian."

Michael Gungor, singer-songwriter

"A must-read for all and a companion guide for a lifelong journey to live generatively. A book full of wisdom, discernment, and humor, *The Road Back to You* creates a path toward home ever so gently and joyfully."

Makoto Fujimura, artist, director, Brehm Center, Fuller Theological Seminary, author of *Silence and Beauty*

THE ROAD BACK TO YOU

AN ENNEAGRAM JOURNEY TO SELF-DISCOVERY

IAN MORGAN CRON

and

SUZANNE STABILE

IVP Books

An imprint of InterVarsity Press
Downers Grove, Illinois

InterVarsity Press
P.O. Box 1400, Downers Grove, IL 60515-1426
ivpress.com
email@ivpress.com

InterVarsity Press® is the book-publishing division of InterVarsity Christian Fellowship/USA®, a movement of students and faculty active on campus at hundreds of universities, colleges and schools of nursing in the United States of America, and a member movement of the International Fellowship of Evangelical Students. For information about local and regional activities, visit intervarsity.org.

Published in association with Creative Trust Literary Group, 210 Jamestown Park, Suite 200, Brentwood, TN, 37027, creativetrust.com.

Cover design: Cindy Kiple
Interior design: Jeanna Wiggins
Images: head illustration: © simon2579/iStockphoto7
        theatric masks: © goce risteski/iStockphoto
        magnifying glass icon: © Alex Belomlinsky/iStockphoto
        dove icon: © Alex Belomlinsky/iStockphoto
        black icons: © Aaltazar/iStockphoto
        color hand icons: © -VICTOR-/iStockphoto
        hand icons: © -VICTOR-/iStockphoto

ISBN 978-0-8308-4619-1 (print)
ISBN 978-0-8308-9327-0 (digital)

Printed in the United States of America ∞

Library of Congress Cataloging-in-Publication Data
Names: Cron, Ian Morgan, 1960- author.
Title: The road back to you : an Enneagram journey to self-discovery / Ian
    Morgan Cron and Suzanne Stabile.
Description: Downers Grove : InterVarsity Press, 2016. | Includes
    bibliographical references.
Identifiers: LCCN 2016036470 (print) | LCCN 2016037719 (ebook) | ISBN
    9780830846191 (hardcover : alk. paper) | ISBN 9780830893270 (eBook)
Subjects: LCSH: Personality--Religious aspects--Christianity. | Typology
    (Psychology)--Religious aspects--Christianity. | Enneagram.
Classification: LCC BV4597.57 .C76 2016 (print) | LCC BV4597.57 (ebook) | DDC
    248.4--dc23
LC record available at https://lccn.loc.gov/2016036470

P	26	25	24												
Y	34	33	32	31	30	29	28	27	26	25	24	23	22	21	20	19

Grant, Lord, that I may know myself
that I may know thee.

AUGUSTINE

Ian

To Anne, Cailey, Aidan, Maddie and Paul, with love

And to Wendell and Ella, my beloved companions

Suzanne

To Giuseppe, my love

And to Joey, Jenny, Joel and BJ, our hope

Contents

1

A CURIOUS THEORY
OF UNKNOWN ORIGIN

One Saturday morning, my cell phone rang at 7:00 a.m. Only one person in the world dares call me at that hour.

"Is this my youngest son, Ian?" my mother said, pretending to be unsure she'd called the right number.

"Yes, it's me," I said, playing along.

"What are you working on?" she asked.

At that moment I wasn't working on anything. I was standing in the kitchen in my boxers wondering why my Nespresso was making end-of-life noises and imagining all the sad ways an early morning conversation with my mother could end if my coffeemaker broke and I was deprived of my day's first cup.

"I'm thinking about writing a primer on the Enneagram," I said, gratefully watching a black stream of coffee love fill my mug.

"The sonogram?" she shot back.

"No, I said the—"

"The anagram?" she said, firing a second round before I could stop her.

"Enneagram. *Enneagram!*" I repeated.

"What's the any-a-gram?" she said.

My mother is eighty-two years old. For sixty-seven of those years she has smoked Pall Malls, successfully avoided exercise and eaten bacon with impunity. She has never needed glasses or a hearing aid and is so spry and mentally acute you'd think nicotine and inactivity were the keys to a long and happy life. She'd heard what I said the first time.

I smiled and continued with one of my Enneagram elevator speeches. "The Enneagram is an ancient personality typing system. It helps people understand who they are and what makes them tick," I said.

There was a long, utterly airless silence on the other end of the phone. I felt like I had been suddenly flung wildly into a black hole in a far-off galaxy.

"Forget the angiogram. Write a book about going to heaven and coming back," she said. "Those authors make money."

I winced. "They also have to die first."

"Details," she purred, and we laughed.

My mother's tepid response to the idea of my writing a book about the Enneagram gave me pause. I had my own reservations about the project as well.

When my grandmother didn't know what to make of something she would say it was "novel." I suspect that's how she'd describe the Enneagram. No one knows for certain when, where or who first came up with the idea for this map of the human personality. What is clear is that it's been a work in progress for a long time. Some trace its origins back to a Christian monk named Evagrius, whose teachings formed the basis for what later became the Seven Deadly Sins, and to the desert mothers and fathers of the fourth century, who used it for spiritual counseling. Some say that elements of the Enneagram also appear in other world religions, including Sufism (the mystical tradition within Islam) and Judaism. In the early 1900s an undeniably strange teacher named George Gurdjieff used the ancient nine-pointed geometric figure, or enneagram, to teach esoteric subjects unrelated to personality types. (I know, I know: if I end the story here I could add Harrison Ford and a monkey and have the backstory for an Indiana Jones movie. But wait, the plot thins!)

In the early 1970s a Chilean named Oscar Ichazo happened upon the Enneagram and made significant contributions, as did one of his pupils, an American-trained psychiatrist named Claudio Naranjo, who developed it further by weaving insights drawn from modern psychology into it. Naranjo brought the Enneagram back to the United States and presented it to a small group of students in California, including a Catholic Jesuit priest and educator on sabbatical from Loyola Seminary named Father Robert Ochs.

Impressed with the Enneagram, Ochs returned to Loyola, where he taught it to seminarians and priests. It soon became known among clergy, spiritual directors, retreat leaders and laypeople as a helpful aid to Christian spiritual formation.

If its sketchy origins weren't enough to spook the mules, there is no scientific evidence that proves the Enneagram is a reliable measurement of personality. Who cares that millions of people claim it's accurate? Grizzly Man thought he could make friends with bears, and we know how that turned out.

So what led me to believe that writing a book about an archaic, historically questionable, scientifically unsupported personality typing system was a good idea?

To answer this question I need to introduce you to a tall, bespectacled monk with knowing eyes and a tenderhearted smile named Brother Dave.

For ten years I served as the founding pastor of a church in Connecticut. I loved the people, but by year seven our average Sunday attendance was running five hundred people, and I was running out of gas. It was clear the church needed a pastor with different gifts, someone who was more a steady-at-the-helm type than an entrepreneurial spirit like me.

For three years I tried everything short of surgery to transform myself into the kind of leader I thought the church needed and wanted me to be, but the project was doomed from the start. The harder I tried, the worse things became. I made more missteps than a guy running through a minefield wearing clown shoes. There was no shortage of confusion, hurt feelings and misunderstandings by the time I left. For me, the end was heartbreaking.

Following my departure I felt disillusioned and confused. Eventually a concerned friend encouraged me to see Br. Dave, a seventy-year-old Benedictine monk and spiritual director.

I first laid eyes on Br. Dave, in his black habit and sandals, standing on the grass-covered roundabout at the end of the monastery driveway waiting to greet me. Everything from the way he used both his hands to grasp mine to the way he smiled and said, "Welcome, traveler, can I make you coffee?" told me I'd come to the right place.

There are monks who pass their days in their monastery's gift shop selling votive candles and giant wheels of homemade cheese, but Br. Dave isn't one of them. He is a wise spiritual director who knows when to console and when to confront.

During our first few sessions Br. Dave listened patiently as I rehearsed the litany of miscalculations and mistakes I'd made in my ministry that in hindsight baffled me. Why had I said and done so many things that seemed right at the time but, looking back, were clearly senseless and at times hurtful to myself and others? How could someone have that many blind spots and still be allowed to drive a car? I felt like a stranger to myself.

By our fourth session I had begun to sound like a lost, half-crazed hiker looking for the path out of a forest while loudly debating with himself how the heck he came to be lost in the first place.

"Ian," Br. Dave said, interrupting my meander, "why are you here?"

"I'm sorry?" I said, as if someone had just tapped me on the shoulder and awakened me from a daydream.

He smiled and leaned forward in his chair. "Why are you here?"

Br. Dave had a knack for posing questions that on the surface seemed almost insultingly simple until you tried to answer them. I looked out the leaded windows lining the wall behind him. Through them I saw a giant elm, the tips of its branches bending toward the earth under the weight of the wind. I struggled to find words to express what I wanted to say but couldn't. The words that came to me weren't my own, but they perfectly captured what I wanted to express.

"I don't really understand myself, for I want to do what is right, but I don't do it. Instead, I do what I hate," I said, surprised a guy who regularly had trouble remembering his cell number could pull Paul's words from Romans 7 out of his hat.

"I want to do what is good, but I don't. I don't want to do what is wrong, but I do it anyway," Br. Dave responded, quoting a verse from the same chapter.

For a moment we sat in silence, considering Paul's words as they spun and glimmered in the air between us like motes in a shaft of sunlight.

"Br. Dave, I don't know who I am or how I got into this mess," I confessed, finally breaking the reverie. "But I'd be grateful if you could help me figure it out."

Br. Dave smiled and sat back in his chair. "Good," he said. "Now we can begin."

At our next meeting Br. Dave asked, "Are you familiar with the Enneagram?"

"A little," I said, shifting in my seat. "But it's kind of a crazy story."

Br. Dave winced and laughed as I told him about my first encounter with it in the early 1990s, when I was a graduate student at a conservative seminary. While on a weekend retreat I came across a copy of Fr. Richard Rohr's book *Discovering the Enneagram: An Ancient Tool for a New Spiritual Journey.* In it Rohr describes the traits and underlying motivations that drive each of the Enneagram's nine basic personality types. Based on my life experience and what I'd learned in my training to become a counselor, Rohr's descriptions of the types were uncannily accurate. I felt sure I had stumbled on an amazing resource for Christians.

On Monday morning I asked one of my professors whether he'd ever heard of it. From the look on his face you'd have thought I'd said *pentagram.* The Bible condemns incantations, sorcery, horoscopes and witches, he said—none of which I recalled being mentioned in the book—and I should throw it away immediately.

At the time I was a young, impressionable evangelical, and though my gut told me my professor's reaction bordered on paranoid, I followed his advice—except the bit about throwing the book in the garbage. For bibliophiles, this is the unpardonable sin that grieves the Holy Spirit. I knew exactly which shelf held my dog-eared copy of Rohr's book in the bookcase in my study.

"It's too bad your professor discouraged you from learning the Enneagram," Br. Dave told me. "It's full of wisdom for people who want to get out of their own way and become who they were created to be."

"What does 'getting out of your own way' entail?" I asked, knowing how many times I'd wanted to do just that in my life but didn't know how.

"It has to do with self-knowledge. Most folks assume they understand who they are when they don't," Br. Dave explained. "They don't question the lens through which they see the world—where it came from, how it's shaped their lives, or even if the vision of reality it gives them is distorted or true. Even more troubling, most people aren't aware of how things that helped them survive as kids are now holding them back as adults. They're asleep."

"Asleep?" I echoed, my face registering confusion.

Br. Dave briefly gazed at the ceiling and frowned. Now he was the one searching for the right combination of words that would unlock the answer to a seemingly simple question.

"What we don't know about ourselves can and will hurt us, not to mention others," he said, pointing his finger at me and then at himself. "As long as we stay in the dark about how we see the world and the wounds and beliefs that have shaped who we are, we're prisoners of our history. We'll continue going through life on autopilot doing things that hurt and confuse ourselves and everyone around us. Eventually we become so accustomed to making the same mistakes over and over in our lives that they lull us to sleep. We need to wake up."

Waking up. There wasn't anything I wanted more.

"Working with the Enneagram helps people develop the kind of self-knowledge they need to understand who they are and why they see and relate to the world the way they do," Br. Dave continued. "When that happens you can start to get out of your own way and become more of the person God created you to be."

After learning his afternoon appointment had canceled, Br. Dave spent extra time with me to talk about the importance of self-knowledge on the spiritual path. How, as John Calvin put it, "without knowledge of self there is no knowledge of God."

"For centuries great Christian teachers have said knowing yourself is just as important as knowing God. Some people will say that's feel-good psychology when actually it's just good theology," he said.

For a moment I thought about all the Bible teachers and pastors I knew who had done things that had blown up their lives and their ministries, often on an epic scale, because they didn't know themselves or the human capacity for self-deceit. They studied and knew the Bible inside and out, but not themselves. I thought of how many Christian marriages I'd seen fall apart largely because neither spouse understood the inner splendor and brokenness of their own souls.

Then I thought about myself. I had always believed I was more self-aware than the average person, but if the last three years had taught me anything it was that I had plenty of growing to do in the self-knowledge department.

Br. Dave looked at his watch and slowly stood up. "I'm away leading retreats for the next month," he announced, stretching to get the blood flowing again after our nearly two-hour seated conversation. "In the meantime, dust off your copy of Rohr's book and reread it. You'll appreciate how he looks at the Enneagram more through the lens of Christian spirituality than psychology. I'll email you the names of a few other books you can read as well."

"I really can't thank you enough," I said, rising from my chair and slinging my backpack over my shoulder.

"We'll have plenty to discuss the next time we meet," Br. Dave promised, embracing me before opening his office door to let me out. "God's peace!" I heard him call down the hallway after me.

Since I was on a long-overdue three-month sabbatical with more time than I knew what to do with, I took Br. Dave's advice to heart and threw myself into learning the Enneagram. For weeks, nearly every morning I walked to the coffee bar at the end of our block and pored over the books he had recommended, taking notes in my journal. At night, I gave a report of everything I was learning from the Enneagram to my wife, Anne. Intrigued, she began to read up on it as well. In that season of our lives together, we had some of the richest, most meaningful conversations in all of our marriage.

Do we *really* know ourselves? How much does our past interfere with our present? Do we see the world through our eyes or through those of the children we were? What are the hidden wounds and misguided beliefs we pick up as kids that continue to secretly govern our lives from the shadows? And how exactly would wrestling with questions like these help us better know God?

These were some of the questions I eagerly lobbed at Br. Dave when he returned from his travels. Sitting in his office, I described for him a handful of the many "aha" moments I had experienced while studying the Enneagram.

"How did you feel when you discovered your type?" Br. Dave asked.

"Well, it wasn't all 'hats and horns,'" I said. "I learned some painful things about myself."

Brother Dave turned around and grabbed a book off his desk and flipped to a page marked by a red sticky flag. "To know oneself is, above all, to know what one lacks. It is to measure oneself against Truth, and not the other way around. The first product of self-knowledge is humility," he said.

"That sums it up pretty well," I said, chuckling.

"It's Flannery O'Connor," Br. Dave said, closing the book and placing it back on his desk. "There's not a lot she doesn't sum up well."

"And Anne?" he continued. "What's it been like for her?"

"One night she read a description of her type to me in bed and she cried," I said. "She's always struggled to find words to describe what it's like to live inside her skin. The Enneagram's been a gift to her."

"Sounds like you're both off to a good start," Br. Dave said.

"It's been incredible. What we've learned from the Enneagram so far has already begun changing the way we think about marriage, friendships and parenting," I said.

"Just remember, it's only one tool to help you deepen your love for God and others," Br. Dave cautioned. "There are plenty of others. What's important is the more you and Anne grow in self-knowledge, the more you'll become aware of your need for God's grace. Not to mention, you'll have more compassion for yourselves and other people."

"I want to read you this Thomas Merton quote I found," I said, leafing through the pages of my journal.

Br. Dave rubbed his hands together and nodded. "Ah, Merton, now you're swimming in deep waters," he smiled.

"Here it is," I said, finding the page where I had written down the quote. I cleared my throat. "Sooner or later we must distinguish between what we are not and what we are. We must accept the fact that we are not what we would like to be. We must cast off our false, exterior self like the cheap and showy garment that it is . . ." I slowed, surprised by the knot in my throat that was making it hard for me to continue.

"Go on," Br. Dave said quietly.

I took a deep breath. "We must find our real self, in all its elemental poverty, but also in its great and very simple dignity: created to be the child of God, and capable of loving with something of God's own sincerity and his unselfishness."

I closed my journal and looked up, flushing from embarrassment at how emotional I had become.

Br. Dave tilted his head to one side. "What was it Merton said that moved you?"

I sat quietly, uncertain how to answer. The monastery's church bells rang outside, calling the monks to prayer.

"I feel like I've been asleep for a long time, but maybe now I'm beginning to wake up," I said. "At least I hope so."

Whenever I said something Br. Dave thought was significant he'd pause to close his eyes and reflect on it. This was one of those times.

Br. Dave opened his eyes. "Before you go, can I pray a blessing for you?" he said.

"Sure," I replied, sliding forward in my chair to get close enough for Br. Dave to wrap both his hands around mine.

May you recognize in your life the presence, power, and light of your soul.

May you realize that you are never alone, that your soul in its brightness and belonging connects you intimately with the rhythm of the universe.

May you have respect for your individuality and difference.

May you realize that the shape of your soul is unique, that you have a special destiny here, that behind the façade of your life there is something beautiful and eternal happening.

May you learn to see your self with the same delight, pride, and expectation with which God sees you in every moment.

"Amen," Br. Dave said, squeezing my hands.

"Let it be so," I whispered, squeezing his hands in return.

Br. Dave's blessing made a difference in my life. Over the years my work with the Enneagram has helped me to see myself "with the same delight, pride, and expectation with which God sees me in every moment." Learning and now teaching the Enneagram has shown me something of the "crooked timber" from which my and others people's hearts are made. The self-understanding I have gained from it has helped me put an end to a few childish ways and become a more spiritual adult. I'm certainly not there yet, but now and again I sense the immediacy of God's grace and for an instant catch a glimpse of the person I was created to be. In the spiritual life that's no small thing.

A few years after my encounter with Br. Dave I accepted an invitation from a woman named Suzanne Stabile to speak at a conference she was hosting at Brite Divinity School. We instantly connected and knew that if left unsupervised by responsible adults, we could get into all kinds of trouble if we became friends.

So we became friends.

When Suzanne told me our mutual friend Richard Rohr had been her spiritual mentor for years and had personally trained her in the Enneagram, I became curious and decided to attend one of her workshops. After an hour of listening to her lecture, I knew Suzanne wasn't just an Enneagram teacher—she was a ninja-level-

Mr. Miyagi-from-*The Karate-Kid* kind of Enneagram teacher. To my good fortune Suzanne picked up where Br. Dave had left off in my life years earlier, kindly taking me on the next leg of my journey toward understanding and applying the wisdom of the Enneagram to my life as a Christian.

Many of the insights and anecdotes on these pages were taken from Suzanne's lectures, while others come from my own life and from what I have learned over the years by attending workshops and studying countless books by renowned Enneagram teachers and pioneers such as Russ Hudson, Richard Rohr, Helen Palmer, Beatrice Chestnut, Roxanne Howe-Murphy and Lynette Sheppard, to name a few. More than anything, however, this book is the product of my and Suzanne's deep affection and respect for one another. It's the only way we know how to throw our two cents of experience and knowledge toward the effort to create a kinder, more compassionate world. We hope it succeeds. If it doesn't, well, we still had a blast doing it.

To be clear, I am not a foamy-mouthed Enneagram zealot. I do not stand uncomfortably close to people at cocktail parties and tell them I was able to guess their Enneagram number based on their choice of footwear. People who do that are an evil begging to be overcome.

But even if I'm not a fanatic, I am a grateful student. To borrow a quote from the British mathematician George Box, "All models are wrong, but some are useful." That's how I see the Enneagram. It is not infallible or inerrant. It is not the be-all and end-all of Christian spirituality. At best, it is an imprecise model of personality . . . but it's *very useful.*

That said, here's my advice. If you find that this book supports you on your spiritual path, great. If not, don't throw it away. Put it on your bookshelf instead. It might come in handy one day. Life hands us a challenging syllabus. We need all the help we can get.

2

FINDING YOUR TYPE

Neuroscientists have determined the brain's dorsolateral prefrontal cortex is associated with decision making and cost-benefit assessments. If MRI brain scans had been performed on my friends and me one summer's night when we were fifteen, they would have revealed a dark spot indicating a complete absence of activity in this region of our brains.

That particular Saturday night a group of us got the brilliant idea that streaking a golf banquet at an exclusive country club in my hometown of Greenwich, Connecticut, was a wise decision. Other than certain arrest for indecent exposure, there was only one problem: Greenwich isn't a big town, and it was likely someone we knew would recognize us. After several minutes of deliberation we decided our friend Mike should run home and return with ski masks for each of us.

And so at roughly 9:00 p.m. on a warm August night, six naked boys in ski masks, several of which were adorned with pom-poms, sprinted like startled gazelles through a beautiful oak-paneled room full of bankers and heiresses. The men clapped and cheered for us while the bejeweled women sat frozen in shock. We had hoped for the opposite reaction, but there was not ample time to stop and express our disappointment.

And that would have been the end of it if it weren't for my mother. "What did you and the guys do last night?" she asked the next morning as I walked into the kitchen and rummaged through the fridge.

"Not much. We hung out at Mike's, then crashed around midnight."

My mother is normally chatty, so I was puzzled when she didn't ask how my friends were doing or what my plans were for the rest of the day. I instantly had an uneasy feeling.

"What did you and Dad do last night?" I said brightly.

"We went as guests of the Dorfmanns to their club's golf banquet," she replied in a tone that was one part sugar, one part steel.

Most people don't ever anticipate that a sudden change in cabin pressure might occur in their home, triggering the hope that an oxygen mask would fall from somewhere overhead to replace the air that shock has just sucked out of their lungs.

"A ski mask?" she demanded, her voice rising as she strolled toward me like an angry Irish cop patting his truncheon in the palm of his hand. *"A ski mask?"*

The tip of her nose was no more than an inch from my own. "I could pick your scrawny butt out of a lineup in the dark," she whispered menacingly.

I tensed, wondering what was coming next, but the storm passed as abruptly as it rolled in. My mother's face relaxed into a sly grin. She turned on her heels and said over her shoulder as she walked out of the kitchen, "You're lucky your father thought it was funny."

This was not the first time I wore a mask to protect myself—far from it.

Human beings are wired for survival. As little kids we instinctually place a mask called personality over parts of our authentic self to protect us from harm and make our way in the world. Made up of innate qualities, coping strategies, conditioned reflexes and defense mechanisms, among lots of other things, our personality helps us know and do what we sense is required to please our parents, to fit in and relate well to our friends, to satisfy the expectations of our culture and to get our basic needs met. Over time our adaptive strategies become increasingly complex. They get triggered so predictably, so often and so automatically that we can't tell where they end and our true natures begin. Ironically, the term *personality* is derived from the Greek word for mask (*persona*), reflecting our tendency to confuse the masks we wear with our true selves, even long after the threats of early childhood have passed. Now we no longer have a personality; our personality has us! Now, rather than protect our defenseless hearts against the inevitable wounds and losses of childhood, our personalities—which we and others experience as the ways we predictably think, feel, act, react, process information and see the world—limit or imprison us.

Worst of all, by overidentifying who we are with our personality we forget or lose touch with our authentic self—the beautiful essence of who we are. As Frederick Buechner so poignantly describes it, "The original, shimmering self gets buried so deep that most of us end up hardly living out of it at all. Instead we live out all the other selves, which we are constantly putting on and taking off like coats and hats against the world's weather."

Though I'm a trained counselor, I don't know exactly how, when or why this occurs, only that this idea of having lost connection with my true self rings true with my experience. How many times while spying my children play or while gazing up at the moon in a reflective moment have I felt a strange nostalgia for something or someone I lost touch with long ago? Buried in the deepest precincts of being I sense there's a truer, more luminous expression of myself, and that as long as I remain estranged from it I will never feel fully alive or whole. Maybe you have felt the same.

The good news is we have a God who would know our scrawny butt anywhere. He remembers who we are, the person he knit together in our mother's womb, and he wants to help restore us to our authentic selves.

Is this the language of the therapeutic under the guise of theology? No. Great Christian thinkers from Augustine to Thomas Merton would agree this is one of the vital spiritual journeys apart from which no Christian can enjoy the wholeness that is their birthright. As Merton put it, "Before we can become who we really are, we must become conscious of the fact that the person who we think we are, here and now, is at best an impostor and a stranger." Becoming conscious is where the Enneagram comes in.

The goal of understanding your Enneagram "type" or "number"— the terms are used interchangeably in this book—is not to delete and replace your personality with a new one. Not only is this not possible, it would be a bad idea. You need a personality or you won't get asked to prom. The purpose of the Enneagram is to develop self-knowledge and learn how to recognize and dis-identify with the parts of our personalities that limit us so we can be reunited with our truest and best selves, that "pure diamond, blazing with the invisible light of heaven," as Thomas Merton said. The point of it is self-understanding and growing beyond the self-defeating dimensions of our personality, as well as improving relationships and growing in compassion for others.

THE NINE PERSONALITY TYPES

The Enneagram teaches that there are nine different personality styles in the world, one of which we naturally gravitate toward and adopt in childhood to cope and feel safe. Each type or number has a distinct way of seeing the world and an underlying motivation that powerfully influences how that type thinks, feels and behaves.

If you're like I was, you will immediately object to the suggestion that there are only nine basic personality types on a planet of more than seven billion people. A single visit to the paint aisle at Home Depot to help an indecisive spouse find "that perfect red" for the bathroom walls might quell your remonstrations. As I recently learned, there are *literally* an infinite number of variations of the color red from which you can select to brighten your bathroom and wreck your marriage at the same time. In the same way, though we all adopt one (and only one) of these types in childhood, there are an infinite number of expressions of each number, some of which might present in a similar way to yours and many of which will look nothing like you on the exterior—but you are all still variations of the same primary color. So don't worry, Mom didn't lie. You are still her special little snowflake.

The Enneagram takes its name from the Greek words for nine (*ennea*) and for a drawing or figure (*gram*). It is a nine-pointed geometric figure that illustrates nine different but interconnected personality types. Each numbered point on the circumference is connected to two others by arrows across the circle, indicating their dynamic interaction with one another.

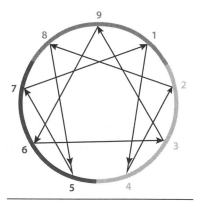

Figure 1. The Enneagram diagram

If you haven't already jumped ahead in this book to begin figuring out which number you are, figure 1 is a snapshot of the diagram. I've also listed the names and a quick description of each Enneagram number. For the record, no personality type is better or worse than another, each has its own strengths and weaknesses, and none is gender-biased.

TYPE ONE: The Perfectionist. Ethical, dedicated and reliable, they are motivated by a desire to live the right way, improve the world, and avoid fault and blame.

TYPE TWO: The Helper. Warm, caring and giving, they are motivated by a need to be loved and needed, and to avoid acknowledging their own needs.

TYPE THREE: The Performer. Success-oriented, image-conscious and wired for productivity, they are motivated by a need to be (or appear to be) successful and to avoid failure.

TYPE FOUR: The Romantic. Creative, sensitive and moody, they are motivated by a need to be understood, experience their oversized feelings and avoid being ordinary.

TYPE FIVE: The Investigator. Analytical, detached and private, they are motivated by a need to gain knowledge, conserve energy and avoid relying on others.

TYPE SIX: The Loyalist. Committed, practical and witty, they are worst-case-scenario thinkers who are motivated by fear and the need for security.

TYPE SEVEN: The Enthusiast. Fun, spontaneous and adventurous, they are motivated by a need to be happy, to plan stimulating experiences and to avoid pain.

TYPE EIGHT: The Challenger. Commanding, intense and confrontational, they are motivated by a need to be strong and avoid feeling weak or vulnerable.

TYPE NINE: The Peacemaker. Pleasant, laid back and accommodating, they are motivated by a need to keep the peace, merge with others and avoid conflict.

Maybe now you're starting to get an idea of which of the nine types you belong to (or which one explains your seventy-year-old uncle who still dresses up like Yoda and attends Star Wars conventions). But the Enneagram is more than a piddling list of clever type names, so that's just the beginning. In the following chapters we'll learn not only about each number in turn but also about how those numbers relate to others. Don't be discouraged if the terminology or the diagram, with its

> "A humble self-knowledge is a surer way to God than a search after deep learning."
>
> **THOMAS À KEMPIS**

lines and arrows ricocheting around, looks confusing. I promise it will make sense to you in short order.

TRIADS

The nine numbers on the Enneagram are divided into three triads—three in the Heart or Feeling Triad, three in the Head or Fear Triad, and three in the Gut or Anger Triad. Each of the three numbers in each triad is driven in different ways by an emotion related to a part of the body known as a center of intelligence. Basically, your triad is another way of describing how you habitually take in, process and respond to life.

The Anger or Gut Triad (8, 9, 1). These numbers are driven by anger—Eight externalizes it, Nine forgets it, and One internalizes it. They take in and respond to life instinctually or "at the gut level." They tend to express themselves honestly and directly.

The Feeling or Heart Triad (2, 3, 4). These numbers are driven by feelings—Twos focus outwardly on the feelings of others, Threes have trouble recognizing their own or other people's feelings, and Fours concentrate their attention inwardly on their own feelings. They each take in and relate to life from their heart and are more image-conscious than other numbers.

The Fear or Head Triad (5, 6, 7). These numbers are driven by fear—Five externalizes it, Six internalizes it, and Seven forgets it. They take in and relate to the world through the mind. They tend to think and plan carefully before they act.

Chapter order. Speaking of triads, if you look at the table of contents you will notice we have chosen not to describe the types in numerical order but to group and discuss them in the context of their respective triads: Eight, Nine and One are together; then Two, Three and Four; and finally Five, Six and Seven. The reason we chose to order the chapters like this is to help you see the important ways in which each number compares to its fellow "triadic roommates." If anything, this will not only make the Enneagram easier to understand but also aid you in your search for your number.

WING, STRESS AND SECURITY NUMBERS

One of the things I love about the Enneagram is that it recognizes and takes into account the fluid nature of the personality, which is constantly adapting as circumstances change. There are times when it's in a healthy space, times when it's in an okay space, or times when it's downright nuts. The point is, it's always moving up and down on a spectrum ranging from healthy to average to unhealthy depending on where you are and what's happening. At the beginning of each chapter I'll briefly describe in broad terms how each number typically thinks, feels and acts when they're camped out in a healthy, average and unhealthy space within their type.

Look at the Enneagram diagram and you'll see that each number has a dynamic relationship with four other numbers. Each number touches the two on either side, as well as the two at the other end of the arrows. These four other numbers can be seen as resources that give you access to their traits or "juice" or "flavor," as I like to say. While your motivation and number never change, your behavior can be influenced by these other numbers, so much so that you can even look like one of them from time to time. As you'll see in each chapter, you can learn to move deliberately around the circle, using these for extra support as needed.

Wing numbers. These are the numbers on either side of your number. You may lean toward one of these two wing numbers and pick up some of its characteristic energy and traits. For example, my friend Doran is a Four (the Romantic) with a Three wing (the Performer). He is more outgoing and more inclined to perform for recognition than a Four with a Five wing (the Investigator), who is more introverted and withdrawing.

Stress and security numbers. Your stress number is the number your personality moves toward when you are overtaxed, under fire, or in the paint aisle at Home Depot with an equivocating friend or partner. It's indicated by the arrow pointing *away* from your number on the Enneagram diagram in figure 2.

For example, normally happy-go-lucky Sevens move toward and take on the negative qualities of the One (the Perfectionist) in stress. They can become less easygoing and adopt more black-and-white thinking. It's important for you to know the number that you go to in stress so that when you catch it activating you can make better choices and take care of yourself.

Your security number indicates the type your personality moves toward and draws energy and resources from when you're feeling secure. It is indicated by the arrow pointing *toward* your number on the Enneagram. For example, Sevens take on the positive qualities of Five when they're feeling secure. That means they can let go of their need for excess and embrace the notion that less is more.

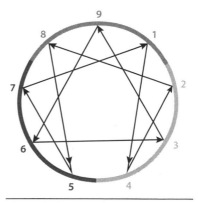

Figure 2. Stress and security arrows

Spiritually speaking, it's a real advantage to know what happens to your type and the number it naturally goes to in stress. It's equally valuable to learn the positive qualities of the number you instinctively move toward in security as well. Once you become familiar with this material you can know and catch yourself when you're heading in the direction of a breakthrough or a breakdown, and make wiser choices than in the past. There's a lot to this topic of security and stress, but because this book is a primer we'll only cover the basics. Just know there is much more to learn about it.

DISCOVER YOUR DEADLY SIN

It may sound like something from a medieval morality play, but each number has a deadly sin associated with it, and in each chapter Suzanne and I will be diving deeper into what that looks like. For some, the word *sin* evokes terrible memories and feelings. Sin as a theological term has been weaponized and used against so many people that it's hard to address the subject without knowing you're possibly hurting someone who has "stood on the wrong end of the preacher's barrel," so to speak.

> "It is my belief no man ever understands quite his own artful dodges to escape from the grim shadow of self-knowledge."
>
> *JOSEPH CONRAD*

But as a weathered sinner and recovering alcoholic with twenty-eight years of sobriety, I know that not facing the reality of our darkness and its sources is a really, really bad idea. Trust me, if you don't, it will eventually come out of your paycheck at the end of the month.

Bearing sensitivities in mind, allow me to offer a definition of *sin* I have found helpful and one we might use together in our conversation. Richard Rohr writes, "Sins are fixations that prevent the energy of life, God's love, from flowing freely. [They are] self-erected blockades that cut us off from God and hence from our own authentic potential." As someone who goes to a church basement several mornings a week to meet with others who need support to stay away from just *one* of my many fixations, this definition rings true. We all have our preferred ways of circumventing God to get what we want, and unless we own and face them head-on they will one day turn our lives into nettled messes.

Every Enneagram number has a unique "passion" or deadly sin that drives that number's behavior. The teachers who developed the Enneagram saw that each of the nine numbers had a particular weakness or temptation to commit one of the Seven Deadly Sins, drawn from the list Pope Gregory composed in the sixth century, plus fear and deceit (along the way a wise person added these two, which is nice because now no one needs to feel left out). Each personality's deadly sin is like an addictive, involuntarily repeated behavior that we can only be free of when we recognize how often we give it the keys to drive our personality. Again, don't think the term *deadly sin* sounds too early Middle Ages to still be relevant. It's timeless and important wisdom! As long as we are unaware of our deadly sin and the way it lurks around unchallenged in our lives we will remain in bondage to it. Learning to manage your deadly sin rather than allowing it to manage you is one of the goals of the Enneagram.

There are other personality typing systems or inventories like the Myers-Briggs or the Five Factor test that are wonderful but exclusively psychological in orientation. There are others that describe and encourage you to embrace who you are, which isn't very helpful if who you are is a jerk. Regardless, only one of these instruments addresses the fact that we are spiritually mottled creatures. The Enneagram is not exclusively psychological, nor is it feel-good, self-help pabulum when taught correctly. (By the way, if my "self" could have helped my "self," don't you think my "self" would have done it by now?) The true purpose of the Enneagram is to reveal to you your shadow side and offer spiritual counsel on how to open it to the transformative light of grace. Coming face-to-face with your deadly sin can be hard, even painful, because it raises to conscious awareness the nastier bits about who we are that we'd rather not think about. "No one should work with the Enneagram if what they seek is flattery. But no one should fail to do so if what they seek is deep knowing of self," as David Benner cautions. So, bravely on!

Here's a list of the Seven Deadly Sins (plus two) and the number to which each correlates, as well as a brief description of them (see figure 3). The descriptions are drawn from Don Riso and Russ Hudson's *The Wisdom of the Enneagram*.

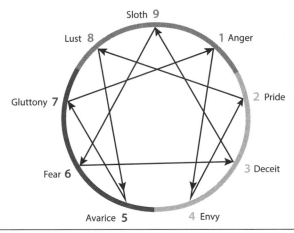

Figure 3. Sins correlating to each number

ONES: Anger. Ones feel a compulsive need to perfect the world. Keenly aware that neither they nor anyone else can live up to their impossibly high standards, they experience anger in the form of smoldering resentment.

TWOS: Pride. Twos direct all their attention and energy toward meeting the needs of others while disavowing having any of their own. Their secret belief that they alone know what's best for others and that they're indispensable reveals their prideful spirit.

THREES: Deceit. Threes value appearance over substance. Abandoning their true selves to project a false, crowd-pleasing image, Threes buy their own performance and deceive themselves into believing they *are* their persona.

FOURS: Envy. Fours believe they are missing something essential without which they will never be complete. They envy what they perceive to be the wholeness and happiness of others.

FIVES: Avarice. Fives hoard those things they believe will ensure they can live an independent, self-sustaining existence. This withholding ultimately leads to their holding back love and affection from others.

SIXES: Fear. Forever imagining worst-case scenarios and questioning their ability to handle life on their own, Sixes turn to authority figures and belief systems rather than God to provide them with the support and security they yearn for.

SEVENS: Gluttony. To avoid painful feelings, Sevens gorge themselves on positive experiences, planning and anticipating new adventures, and entertaining interesting ideas. Never satisfied, the Seven's frenzied pursuit of these distractions eventually escalates to the point of gluttony.

EIGHTS: Lust. Eights lust after intensity. It can be seen in the excessiveness they evidence in every area of life. Domineering and confrontational, Eights present a hard, intimidating exterior to mask vulnerability.

NINES: Sloth. For Nines, sloth refers not to physical but to spiritual laziness. Nines fall asleep to their own priorities, personal development and responsibility for becoming their own person.

THE NINE TYPES IN CHILDHOOD

It's staggering to think how many messages our uncritical minds and hearts pick up and internalize in childhood, and how many hours and dollars we later spend on therapists trying to pick them out of our psyches like burrs from the coat of a sheepdog. Some messages and beliefs we unconsciously take in as kids are life giving, while others wound. Most of us unknowingly surrender our lives to the messages that most perforate our beauty. We should remind ourselves of this more often. We would be kinder to each other if we did.

In the chapters that follow we'll take a look at how each number tends to play out in childhood, with Twos learning to happily give up their Cheez-Its at lunch to buy love and Fives observing the other kids' play before tentatively deciding to join in. These kids are reflecting both their natural tendencies and the mask they are unconsciously hoping will protect them. They are growing into their number.

The good news is that there are healing messages that we can choose to change the direction of our thoughts, beliefs and behaviors. Learning a healing message unique to each number is a useful aid to help us along on our journey back to our true selves, to the wholeness we crave. It can become a salve of compassion for ourselves, teaching us to respond to old patterns by reminding us to let go of the false self we developed to protect ourselves in childhood and to put on the true self.

YOUR TYPE IN RELATIONSHIPS AND AT WORK

I once worked with a person whose self-awareness quotient was so low as to be unquantifiable. His lack of self-knowledge and inability to self-regulate wounded so many of his colleagues that he should have been removed by OSHA as a workplace health and safety hazard.

The truth is, people who lack self-knowledge not only suffer spiritually but professionally as well. I recently read a *Harvard Business Review* article in which the entrepreneur Anthony Tjan writes, "There is one quality that trumps all, evident in virtually every great entrepreneur, manager, and leader. That quality is self-awareness. The best thing leaders can do to improve their effectiveness is to become more aware of what motivates them and their decision-making." Numerous other books and articles on the topic of self-awareness in magazines from *Forbes* to *Fast Company* all say the same thing: *know thyself.*

In this book, we'll look at a few ways the behaviors associated with our particular number can help or hinder us as we perform our work and relate to colleagues. It can also help us in the process of discerning what career path we should pursue, whether we're currently on the right one for us, or whether the professional environment we're currently working in is a good fit based on the strengths and liabilities of our personalities.

God wants you to enjoy and be effective in your work (unless, like my wife, you've chosen to teach eighth grade, in which case you got the pizza you ordered). By expanding self-knowledge and self-awareness, the Enneagram can help you perform better and experience more satisfaction in your vocation, so much so that companies and organizations like Motorola, the Oakland A's baseball team, the CIA and clergy from the Vatican, among many others, have used it to help their people find more joy in their work. Even Stanford University and Georgetown University's business schools have included it in their curriculums.

The Enneagram also offers great insight into how our personality types engage in relationships with partners or friends and what we most need and fear from those interactions. All of us bring some amount of brokenness to our connections with others, but you should understand that every single number on the Enneagram is capable of healthy and life-giving relationships. Every number has its healthy, average and unhealthy range of behaviors. With greater self-awareness, you can help ensure that your typical behaviors land more on the healthy side and don't sabotage your interactions with the people you love the most.

SPIRITUAL FORMATION

> "I love a lot of people, understand none of them."
>
> **FLANNERY O'CONNOR**

"Accepting oneself does not preclude an attempt to become better," observed Flannery O'Connor, and she's right. Your Enneagram number is not like a note from your mother that you can hand the universe whenever you behave badly that says, "To Whom It May Concern, you must excuse my son John. He is a Nine (or whatever John's number might be) and is therefore incapable of acting any better than what you've witnessed him do to date." If anything, once you know your Enneagram number it takes away any excuse you might have for not changing. Now you know too much to cop the "This is just who I am so deal with it" plea.

Recently in a twelve-step meeting I heard someone say, "Insight is cheap." Man, is that ever true! As Fr. Rohr points out, "Information is not transformation." Once you know your type you owe it to yourself and the people you love (or don't love, for that matter) to become a kinder, more compassionate presence in the world. May a pox fall on anyone who reads this book and walks away with no more than something "interesting" to prattle on about at a dinner party. The purpose of the Enneagram is to show us how we can release the paralyzing arthritic grip we've kept on old, self-defeating ways of living so we can open ourselves to experiencing more interior freedom and become our best selves.

At the end of every chapter you will find a spiritual transformation section that offers each type a few suggestions on how they can put what they've learned about themselves to good use. This is helpful information so long as you don't waste your time trying to accomplish any of it apart from the transformative power of God's grace. Anyone who says they're "trying" to be a good Christian right away reveals they have no idea what a Christian is. Christianity is not something you do as much as something that gets done to you. Once you know the dark side of your personality, simply give God consent to do for you what you've never been able to do for yourself, namely, bring meaningful and lasting change to your life.

HOW TO READ EACH CHAPTER AND FIGURE OUT YOUR TYPE

It's tempting, but as you read the chapters that follow, don't try to type yourself solely on the basis of behaviors. At the start of each chapter you will find a list of "I" statements designed to give you a sense of how people of that particular number might describe what it's like to live in their skin. Keep in mind as you read these lists, however, that *your number is not determined by what you do so much as by why you do it.* In other words, don't rely too much on traits to identify your type. Instead, read carefully about the underlying *motivation* that drives the traits or behaviors of each number to see whether it rings true for you. For example, several different numbers might climb the ladder at work, but the reasons they do so are very different: motivated by a compulsive need to improve things, Ones might seek advancement because they've heard only people in top management have the authority to fix the countless imperfections the One can't help fixating on in the company's day-to-day operations; Threes might climb it because getting the corner office is important to them; and Eights might scale the ladder just to see who's stupid enough to try to stop them. Motivation is what matters! To find your number ask yourself why you do the things you do.

It will help you identify your type if, as you read along, you think back to what you were like at age twenty rather than who you are now. Even though your personality type never changes, it's never more florid or clear than in early adulthood when, as James Hollis says, you haven't lived long enough to figure out that you are "the only person who is consistently present in every scene of that long-running drama we call our life"—in other words, the source of most of your problems is you. It's also important to think more about the way you act, think and feel at home.

Look for the type that best describes who you are, not the type you'd like to think you are or have always wanted to be. If given my druthers I'd like to be a charming, happy-go-lucky Seven like Stephen Colbert, but I'm a garden-variety "Bob Dylan" Four minus the talent. (Throughout the book I give examples of famous people for each number. These are guesses on my part, not self-reported by the people themselves.) As Anne Lamott says, "Everyone is screwed up, broken, clingy, and scared," so there's no sense wanting to be differently screwed up than you already are. As you try to figure out your type, it's great to ask your close friends, spouse or spiritual director to read the descriptions and offer their opinions about which type they think sounds most like you—but don't kill the messenger.

If while reading a description you begin to feel squeamish because it's captured your inner world in a way only someone who hacked into the server where you back up your personality could know about, then you're probably zeroing in on your number. When I first read my number I felt humiliated. It's not pleasant to be the rat in a dark kitchen who is so focused on devouring crumbs that he doesn't hear the stealthy homeowners approaching and therefore doesn't have time to take cover before they suddenly switch on the light and catch the rat in the act with a bagel in its mouth. On the other hand I felt consoled. I didn't know there were other rats like me. So if this happens, don't despair. Remember each number has its assets and liabilities, blessings and blights. The embarrassment will pass, but in the words of novelist David Foster Wallace, "The truth will set you free, but not until it's done with you."

Don't expect to identify with every single feature of your number—you won't. Just be on the lookout for the one that comes closest to describing who you are. If it's any comfort, it takes some people several months to explore the numbers and gather feedback from others before they feel confident in identifying their type.

I often hear beginning students of the Enneagram taking what they're learning about other types and turning it into a weapon to dismiss or ridicule other people. It gets my hackles up when I hear someone say to another person something akin to, "Oh you're so Six" or "Stop being such a Three," particularly when the person they're saying it to has no idea what the Enneagram is. *The Enneagram should only be used to build others up and help them advance on their journey toward wholeness and God. Period.* We hope you take this to heart.

A few of the type descriptions might also sound suspiciously reminiscent of a family member, coworker or friend. You might feel tempted to call your sister to tell her you now understand the reason she made your childhood a living hell had more to do with her personality type than demonic possession as previously believed. Don't do this. Everyone will hate you.

"I don't want to be pigeonholed or put in a box." People express this concern to Suzanne and me all the time. Fear not! The Enneagram doesn't put you in a box. It shows you the box you're already in and how to get out of it. So that'll be good, right?

Now this is very important: At times, you will feel that we're focusing far too much on the negative rather than the positive qualities of each number. We are, but only to help you more easily discover your type. In our experience, people identify more readily with what's not working in their personalities than with what is. As Suzanne likes to say, "We don't know ourselves by what we get right; we know ourselves by what we get wrong." Try not to get all pouty.

Finally, have a sense of humor and be compassionate toward yourself and others.

The universe is undemocratic. A man in a white lab coat holding a clipboard didn't appear at the moment of your conception to inquire whether you preferred to be genetically matched with Pope Francis or Sarah Palin. You didn't pick your parents, your lunatic siblings or the place you occupy in the family birth order. You didn't choose the town where you were born or the side of the track on which your childhood home sat. That we were not consulted about these matters has long been a source of contention between God and me. But over time I've learned that in addition to sins born of the ego's desire to have everyone in the world organize their lives around ours, we face many challenges that are not of our own making but which we are responsible to do something about. Either way, always maintain a compassionate stance toward yourself as God does. Self-contempt will never produce lasting, healing change in our lives, only love. This is the physics of the spiritual universe, for which we should all be grateful and say, "Amen!"

And so as Br. Dave would say, "Now we can begin."

WHAT IT'S LIKE TO BE AN EIGHT

(You don't understand why we're starting with Eights? Reread page 27.)

1. I have been told that I'm too blunt and aggressive.

2. Doing things halfway is not my spiritual gift.

3. I enjoy a good verbal skirmish, just to see what others are made of.

4. In relationships that matter to me I insist on being honest about conflicts and staying in the fight till things are worked out.

5. It's hard for me to trust people.

6. Justice is worth fighting for.

7. I can sniff out other people's weakness the first time I meet them.

8. Saying no isn't a problem for me.

9. I welcome opposition. Bring it.

10. I make decisions fast and from the gut.

11. I don't like it when people beat around the bush.

12. I'm wary of people who are super nice.

13. When I walk into a room I know immediately who has the most power.

14. I don't have much respect for people who don't stand up for themselves.

15. One of my mottos is "A good offense is better than a good defense."

16. Don't mess with the people I love.

17. I know I'm respected. But sometimes I want to be loved.

18. I have no problem confronting a bully.

19. If God wanted people to wear their hearts on their sleeve, he would have put it there.

20. Under my tough exterior is a tender, loving heart.

3

TYPE EIGHT

The Challenger

Lead me, follow me, or get out of my way.

GENERAL GEORGE S. PATTON JR.

Healthy Eights are great friends, exceptional leaders and champions of those who cannot fight on their own behalf. They have the intelligence, courage and stamina to do what others say can't be done. They have learned to use power in the right measure at the right times, and they are capable of collaborating and valuing the contributions of others. They understand vulnerability and even embrace it at times.

Average Eights tend to be steamrollers more than diplomats. They are dualistic thinkers, so people are good or bad, opinions are right or wrong, and the future is bright or bleak. They prefer to lead, struggle to follow and use aggression to emotionally protect themselves. Many Eights are leaders, and others follow them with little or no hesitation. They have little patience with people who are indecisive or who don't pull their weight.

Unhealthy Eights are preoccupied with the idea that they are going to be betrayed. Suspicious and slow to trust others, they resort to revenge when wronged. They believe they can change reality, and they make their own rules and expect others to follow them. Eights in this space destroy as much as they create, believing the world is a place where people are objects to be used and contributions from others have little or no lasting value.

When we first moved to Nashville our family was invited to a dinner party at the home of a new neighbor. Over dinner my then thirteen-year-old son Aidan began to talk about a story he'd heard and enjoyed on the way home from school on the NPR show *All Things Considered*. Aidan wasn't three sentences into describing the premise of the story when a middle-aged man across the table interrupted him by booming out, "The only people who listen to NPR are latte-drinking, skinny-jean-wearing, clove-cigarette-smoking hipsters."

Aidan's eyes grew wide as his face reddened. He hadn't yet learned that our community is for the most part politically conservative, and some of its residents regard NPR as no more than a propaganda machine for Ivy-League-educated communists. The neighbor then launched into a doozy of a tirade about left-wingers inventing global warming to destroy capitalism, the Supreme Court's plan to impose sharia law, and something about his pit bull's right to carry a handgun in the dog park.

An excruciating silence fell on the room. I was about to say something on Aidan's behalf when, from the vicinity where my daughter Cailey was sitting, I heard the unmistakable clearing of the throat that I knew translated to "Pilot to bombardier, open bomb bay doors." She was directly over her target and preparing to drop her rhetorical ordnance. I was about to yell, "Run, Bambi, run!" but there was no time. I commended the man's soul to God.

At the time Cailey was a twenty-two-year-old senior at Middlebury College, one of the better liberal arts colleges in the country.

This girl is smart as a whip, and she doesn't suffer fools gladly, particularly fools who pick on people she loves.

Cailey picked up her napkin from her lap, dabbed the corners of her mouth, calmly folded and placed it next to her plate, then turned to face the man who had smacked down her younger brother. "You're kidding, right?" she said, glaring at him like a panther marking its prey.

The man's eyebrows made a retreat up his forehead. "I'm sorry?" he responded, sadly unaware that the gates of hell were now unguarded.

Cailey turned to the rest of us at the table and gestured toward the man the way a circus ringmaster gestures to a clown about to be shot out of a cannon: "Friends, I give you another wingnut who uncritically believes everything he hears on conservative talk radio."

The man shifted uncomfortably in his chair and sniffed. "Young lady, I—"

Cailey held up her hand to the man's face like a cop stopping traffic and proceeded to uncover and shred every weakness in his argument. It was an unrelenting fusillade of criticism, after a few minutes of which I felt a moral obligation to step in and stop.

"Thank you, Cailey," I said.

"Sir, do us all a favor and have a point the next time you shoot your mouth off," she said, finishing the man off with a stinging flourish. She then unfolded her napkin and returned it to her lap. "Would you please pass the salt?" she said, licking her paws.

Cailey is an Eight on the Enneagram.

THE EIGHT'S DEADLY SIN

Eights are called Challengers because they're aggressive, confrontational, high-voltage people who approach life the way Alaric and his Visigoths approached Rome: they sack it.

The deadly sin of the Eight is *lust,* but not in the sexual sense. Eights lust after intensity—they are high-voltage human dynamos who want to be wherever the action and energy are, and if they can't find any, they'll cook it up. Eights have more energy than any other number on the Enneagram. They are fiery, zestful, earthy, full-throttle people who drink life down to the dregs and then slam their glass down and order a second round for everyone else at the bar.

Eights don't need a Marine band to play "Hail to the Chief" to let a group of people know they've arrived. When Eights walk into a room you feel their presence before you see them. Their larger-than-life energy doesn't fill a space; it *owns* it.

Visualize a men's locker room in which a group of guys is standing around whining about how "challenging" their restorative yoga class was. Then imagine the awe-soaked silence that would fall over them if a towel-clad Dwayne "The Rock" Johnson walked by and glanced their way. You'd have a bunch of guys squinting down at the floor, saying, "Can any of you see my contact lens?"

You get the idea.

FAMOUS EIGHTS
Martin Luther King Jr.
Muhammad Ali
Angela Merkel

Not all Eights speak loudly or karate-chop the air with their hands to drive home a point in conversation; nor are they all physically intimidating people. These are stereotypes, not personality types. The defining feature of an Eight is the overabundance of intense energy they radiate wherever they go. Regardless of whether they are introverts or extroverts, big or small, male or female, liberal or conservative, every Eight I've ever known oozes confidence, fearlessness and strength. Like Kazantzakis's Zorba the Greek, they're juicy people who respond with gusto to whatever life throws their way.

Spiritually healthy, self-aware Eights love to do what others say can't be done. When their energy is harnessed and channeled they can change the course of history. Think Martin Luther King Jr.

On the other hand, a spiritually undeveloped Eight who tests poorly on the self-knowledge scale is someone you want to keep away from the kids. Think Joseph Stalin.

ALL ABOUT EIGHTS OR CHALLENGERS

Anger is the dominant emotion in an Eight's life. They are fiercely independent people whose oppositional energy expresses itself in a need to be strong and go up against power. Eights assume others are untrustworthy until they've proven themselves otherwise. It's no surprise, then, that anger is their go-to emotion. It's so close to the surface that you can sometimes feel like it's radiating off them like a space heater. And because anger is so easy for them to access, an average Eight can be a little too quick to the draw, firing off a few rounds at people without thinking beforehand about the consequences. Their flashes of anger, however, are unconscious defense maneuvers to avoid acknowledging or revealing weakness or vulnerability. Eights use anger like a palisade to hide behind and defend the softer, more tender feelings of the open-hearted, innocent child they once were, the one they don't want others to see.

Eights don't come equipped with dimmers. They are on or off, all in or all out. They "go big or go home." They want to express their animal drives and satisfy their appetite for life without limitations or constraints being placed on them by anybody. This impulsive, all-or-nothing approach to life leaves Eights prone to being overindulgent and excessive. They can overwork, overparty, overeat, overexercise, overspend, over-anything. For an Eight, too much of a good thing is almost enough. As my Eight friend Jack likes to say, "If something's worth doing, it's worth overdoing." (You don't want to play beer pong against Jack. It doesn't end well.)

All this hot-blooded, passionate and combative energy can feel overwhelming and threatening to people who aren't Eights. Most folks go to parties hoping to have fun and talk to interesting people, not to find themselves verbally sparring against the wunderkind captain of the Harvard debate team. Try not to take it personally. As strange as it sounds, what feels like intimidation to you feels like intimacy to an Eight. For them, conflict is connection.

In my experience Eights don't see themselves as angry people. In fact, they're genuinely surprised when they learn other people experience them as intimidating, insensitive and domineering. "Every year during my annual review I'd get the same feedback," Jim, a former Nashville record label executive and Eight told me. "My boss would say when it came to sales I killed it, but my staff consistently complained to him that I was overbearing, gruff and ran roughshod over their ideas. I honestly had no idea that's how people felt around me." Eights see themselves as honest, straight-talking people who aren't afraid to go nose to nose with whatever life throws at them and always leave everything on the field.

Lucky for us, Eights care deeply about justice and fairness. They are fierce advocates for widows, orphans, the poor and the margin-alized. They have no problem speaking truth to power, and they are perhaps the only number on the Enneagram who are brave enough to confront and take down the oppressors and dictators of the world. Go on my daughter Cailey's Facebook page and I guarantee you'll find a photo of her marching in a recent protest to end police brutality, raise the minimum wage or force a university to divest from companies that produce fossil fuels. You'll have to look else-where for cute kitten memes.

Though Eights' concern for justice, fairness and defending the underdog is genuine, there is another drama underway here as well. Having witnessed or experienced the negative consequences of powerlessness as a child, the Eight identifies with the easily preyed upon and rushes to their aid.

Eights' concern for justice is great until they throw on tights and a cape and arrogate to themselves the role of the superhero sent to avenge the defenseless and restore balance to the scales of justice. This is a temptation to Eights who are more often dualistic than non-dualistic thinkers. They see things as black or white, good or bad, fair or unfair. People are friend or foe, weak or strong, streetwise or suckers. In an Eight's mind, you and I have opinions while they have facts. They absolutely believe their viewpoints or positions on issues are irrefutable. They reject taking a nuanced view of anything because not having clarity or absolute certainty about your position represents weakness or—God forbid—cowardice. If you want to try to convince them otherwise, I suggest you pack your pajamas because it's going to be a long night.

Eights can start an argument in an empty house. A good old-fashioned verbal brawl gives them the opportunity to "get big" and disabuse people of any illusion they might previously have held about the Eight being weak. Eights value truth, and there's nothing like a nose-to-nose confrontation to bring it to light. Eights know other people can show their hands in the heat of a fight. A confrontation can expose what's *really* happening behind the scenes, force people's real intentions or hidden agendas into the open, or reveal whether people can stand their ground and be trusted.

Each number has a signature communication style. Knowing the talk style of each number will not only give you insight into other people's types but will help you narrow down your own number as well. The talk style of Eights is *commanding*. Often their sentences are littered with imperatives and end with exclamation marks.

> "You lose nothing when fighting for a cause. In my mind the losers are those who don't have a cause to care about."
>
> **MUHAMMAD ALI**

Whereas most people experience conflict as anything but invigorating, Eights get their energy from it. If conversation at the holiday table takes an unexciting turn, Eights will pull out their phones and secretly check their email under the table. If it stays boring they'll take off their gloves and say something like, "I'd rather throw myself under a bus than live with this president for another four years," then sit back and watch the fun.

EIGHTS AS CHILDREN

So where do these forces of nature come from? A common story Suzanne and I hear from Eights is that something happened in their formative years that required them to prematurely abandon their childlike innocence in order take responsibility for their own lives and often the lives of others. Some Eights were raised in unstable environments or homes where toughness was rewarded with praise. (This does not apply to my own daughter. She grew up in Eden.) Others report they were bullied at school until it became clear they could rely on no one but themselves. These struggles may or may not reflect your experience as a child. Don't reject out of turn the possibility you're an Eight or any other number solely on the basis that you don't identify with a particular childhood story.

Regardless of the root cause, as kids Eights picked up the wounding message that "the world is a hostile place where only the strong survive, and the weak or innocent get emotionally beaten up or betrayed. So put on your armor and never let them see your soft side." Eights worry a lot about betrayal. It's why many of them won't trust more than a small circle of friends over the course of their lives.

As they grew a little older, Eights looked around the sandbox or their home and saw a "might makes right" world in which there were two types of people—those who controlled others and those who submitted. They figured out that weaker kids ended up as followers and vowed, "Not me, pal." You can't tell by looking at them, but Eights don't feel like they have to be the person in control—*they just don't want to be controlled.* (That last sentence is so important that I will set my alarm clock to wake me up to Nickelback's song "Rockstar" every morning for a year if it means you reread and remember that sentence. You'll never fully understand Eights if you don't grasp that distinction.)

One of my favorite stories about Eights as kids involves Suzanne's daughter Joey. When Joey was five, Suzanne got a voicemail message from the head of the daycare center she attended. If you've raised children, you know that a call like this means that your kid is either throwing up in the Lego bucket or is in need of some crucial item that you, woefully pathetic parent that you are, failed to send them to school with. It's also possible you have a serial biter who is not responding to "ongoing positive guidance" that morning and needs their muzzle. In any case, it means you have to go face the principal.

But Suzanne was surprised to discover that the problem wasn't any of these typical scenarios. She learned to her bewilderment that Joey had come in earlier in the week to schedule an appointment with Mrs. Thompson, the director of the daycare.

"Suzanne, as you can imagine, we've *never* had a five-year-old request a formal meeting," Mrs. Thompson explained. "My secretary wasn't sure what to do so she went ahead and scheduled it."

"Why did she want to meet with you?" Suzanne asked.

"Well, Joey walked into my office ahead of me and suggested that we take a seat. I did, but she didn't, so she was eye level with me. She handed me a folder she'd been carrying under her arm and said, 'Thank you for meeting with me, Mrs. Thompson. I have a problem and I tried talking to my teacher about it, but she wasn't much help. I understand that most kids need to take a nap. But I don't. So rather than being bored and made to lie down during that time I have an idea.'"

Mrs. Thompson then handed over Joey's folder containing all her papers—all of which bore gold stars. Joey had brought the folder to Mrs. Thompson as Exhibit A to demonstrate her impeccable credentials and the genius of her plan: since she didn't need a nap and her own papers were flawless, she should be permitted to help the teachers by checking papers during naptime.

"And I can do this for you for only $1.47 an hour," Joey said, straightening her back to bring herself to her full height.

"Suzanne, I can't pay her! It's against the law!" said the director after she had finished the story.

"So did you just tell her no?" Suzanne asked.

The frown of disbelief on her face indicated that Mrs. Thompson had not even considered this possibility. Joey hadn't given her the impression it was an option.

The point of this story is not to show that Eights are bullies and Joey had a leg up on it. (In fact, unless they're very unhealthy, Eights are not characteristically bullies. Bullies act out to compensate and cover their own fears, while Eights aren't afraid of anyone. Because of their concern for justice and desire to instinctively protect and defend the disadvantaged, Eights are more likely to stand up to bullies.) It's to show how deep the wiring of the Eight's number runs. Joey was flexing her Eightness even at the age of five.

Like Joey, kids who are Eights often run ahead of the pack and want to be allowed to act independently. These kids trust themselves more than they trust most adults, and they have plenty of stamina for meeting challenges and getting things done.

Young Eights will get in line when limits are placed on them, but their motive has less to do with pleasing and more with hoping they'll be rewarded with more freedom and independence for good behavior. They don't feel a need to conform, but they know when it's to their advantage to follow the rules. These kids literally take over when it seems that no one else is at the helm, and they usually do a good job—so good a job that when people point to our daughter Cailey as evidence that we must have been reasonably decent parents, we say, "What makes you think we had anything to do with it?"

Unfortunately, the downside of their independence and self-reliance is that these kids can forget their innocence much too early, and it is difficult to reclaim it later in life. They need to recover a little of the open-heartedness that defines childhood for others. They need to remember that time in life when they didn't need to be in charge or control to feel safe, when they could trust others to protect them. They need the lessons that mistakes and weakness teach us: the value of an apology, the experience of forgiveness and the lessons we only learn from following another leader. If their boldness doesn't get shaped and channeled toward becoming a force for good in the course of development, later on it can bloom into full-blown oppositional stances toward the world.

THE CHALLENGER IN RELATIONSHIPS

I love the Eights in my life. I wouldn't trade my relationships with them for anything in the world. This doesn't mean that Eights are easy in relationships, only that the care and energy you have to expend to be their friend or partner is worth it.

Eights want people to challenge them right back. Eights admire strength. They won't respect you if you're not willing to stand toe to toe with them. They want others to be their equals and stand up for what they believe. The last thing you want to do is hoist the white flag when Eights start pounding their chests and trying to push you around.

One night a family friend who is an Eight came over for dinner. Living one door down from my childhood home, Ed watched me grow up from the time I was a baby. I love him like a father, but he can be a lot to handle. Over dessert I mentioned how much I had enjoyed the movie *Birdman*.

"That movie sucked," he announced. "It was too long, the premise was stupid, and Michael Keaton sure isn't what he used to be. Why anyone would think *Birdman* was a good movie is beyond me," he said, waving his fork in the air like a fencing saber.

Like most Eights, Ed lives by the "Fire, Aim, Ready" rule. He's a no-nonsense guy who speaks first and thinks later. Maybe. Over the years I'd learned to peel myself off the pavement and brush myself off after Ed mounted his bulldozer and ran me over this way. But as a student and teacher of the Enneagram I decided to see what would happen if I met him on the field of battle.

"Who are you, Roger freaking Ebert?" I said, mustering my big-boy voice and jabbing my finger across the table at him. "The script was great, the direction was flawless, and I'll bet you fifty bucks Michael Keaton gets nominated for an Academy Award. Why anyone would think that *Birdman* is a bad movie is beyond me."

No one at the table moved. My kids steeled themselves to become orphans. Ed sat back and for a brief moment looked at me curiously.

"Touché," he said, smiling and stabbing his tiramisu.

And that was that.

The group of us returned to normal conversation as if our momentary skirmish had been no more than a brief commercial interruption. That's how it is with Eights. They'll respect you if you hold your ground with them, and once the confrontation is over, it's as if nothing happened.

Eights want the unvarnished truth. Unless you like lengthy estrangements, never lie or send a mixed message to an Eight. You have to tell the truth, the whole truth and nothing but the truth. Information is power, so Eights want to know all the facts. For a case in point, fast forward fifteen years to Suzanne and Joey. Joey was headed home from college when she was involved in a serious car accident that left her with a fractured shoulder, a dislocated hip and nasty bruising. When Suzanne saw Joey just before she went into surgery, she was shocked to see her looking so beat up, every inch of her face pockmarked from rolling in the gravel.

Fighting tears, Joey asked, "Mom, do I look horrible?"

"Yes, sweetheart," Suzanne said, "you do." A gasp went up from the nurses nearby, the kind of gasp that Suzanne tells me women universally recognize as an intentional expression of judgment. The louder the gasp, the deeper the judgment. But Suzanne knew that Eights *always* want the truth, so she didn't paper it over. Eights don't want you to protect them from the facts or coddle them by leaving out the unpleasant details. In an Eight's mind, there's a lot at stake. If they don't know the truth, then they don't know what's really happening, and if they don't know what's really happening, then they're not in control, and not in control is where Eights *never* want to be. If you hold back any relevant information, Eights will feel like you've left them flapping in the wind and dangerously exposed. You don't want to lose an Eight's trust. It takes a long time to get it back, *so always lead with the truth.*

Eights want to be in control. Eights never want to feel like they're not in control. This is one reason they don't often say "I'm sorry." If you tell them they've said or done something that hurt you, they may even make matters worse by accusing you of being too sensitive. When things go wrong Eights who lack self-awareness are super quick to blame others rather than own up and take responsibility for their mistakes. For spiritually immature Eights, expressing remorse or admitting their part in what's gone wrong represents weakness. Eights worry that if they own up and apologize for their behavior, you will bring it up and use it against them in the future. If it's any consolation, when in the silence of their own hearts they realize they've hurt someone they love, some Eights will beat themselves up mercilessly (as long as they're convinced they're wrong).

Remember that Eights are imposing, commanding personalities who need to be "the boss." Unless you put the brakes on they will take charge of possessions, the family social calendar, the TV remote and the checkbook. Because they are so expansive and self-extending, Eights can walk into a room where you're sitting, and within minutes their full-throated voice, larger-than-life gesticulations and unsolicited but emphatically offered opinions will begin to assert control over the environment like an occupying power.

Eights are "Don't complain, don't explain" people. They don't make excuses, and they expect you not to either. If you're in a romantic relationship with an Eight, you have to know who you are and be independent. They don't want you to draft off their energy; they want you to bring your own. They love debates, risky adventures and getting people riled up.

All this excess and intolerance for constraints means Eights need friends and partners who can help keep them in check. As you'll learn, "self-forgetting" is a hallmark of all three numbers in the Anger Triad (8, 9, 1). In addition to forgetting their childhood innocence, one of the things Eights forget is that they're not invincible super humans. Many Eights feel physically bigger and more powerful than they are, so they'll place unreasonable demands on their bodies and put their health and well-being at risk. They'll bristle when you say it, but Eights need to be reminded that moderation is a virtue, not a restraining order.

Eights have a tender side. If you're fortunate enough to have an Eight in your life, you know that beneath all the intensity and anger energy there is a heart brimming with tenderness and love. Eights will step in front of a speeding train or take a bullet to the chest for their small circle of friends.

> "Aggressive fighting for the right is the noblest sport the world affords."
> **THEODORE ROOSEVELT**

Feel honored when an Eight displays tenderness or shares vulnerable thoughts or feelings with you. A big problem for Eights is confusing vulnerability for weakness, so they rarely let down their guard to allow others to see their fragility or their deep desire to be understood and loved. This is why Eights are often attracted to Enneagram feeling types (2, 3, 4), who can help them get in touch with and outwardly express their affection.

Eights are eager to support people who want to realize their potential. They know how to empower and bring out the best in others, and they'll block or tackle to help someone get to where they want to go in life. All they ask is that you show up and give 150 percent of yourself to reaching the goal. If you don't, the once-supportive Eight will move on to find someone else willing to put in the effort.

When Eights are in a healthy space they're a blast. They laugh easily, entertain generously and tell the kind of jokes that make you donkey snort. But they are serious competitors as well. Whether you're playing against them in the finals at Wimbledon or just in a chummy game of croquet on the front lawn, you'll soon discover that Eights hate to lose more than they love to win.

Eights' antagonism can sabotage their relationships. The Enneagram reveals how our solutions are often worse than our problems. By regularly testing authority, being overly blunt and insensitive, acting in a confrontational manner, insisting their perspective is always the right one, or acting impulsively, Eights don't protect themselves from attack, from losing their grip on control or from experiencing emotional harm and betrayal—rather, they invite it.

People can become fed up with feeling pushed around or intimidated by a spiritually immature Eight, and will either walk away from a relationship with them or band together to overthrow them professionally or exclude them socially. Sadly, when this happens it only confirms Eights' worst fears about the dangerous nature of the world, the untrustworthiness of others and the likelihood of betrayal.

Eights are looking for an answer to the question "Can I trust *me* with *you*?" At the end of the day, they want to find someone with whom they can feel safe enough to relax their defenses and reveal their heart.

EIGHTS AT WORK

Eights can be found in any profession. They make phenomenal prosecutors or defense attorneys, coaches, missionaries, business people and organization builders. Because they like to be in charge, free from limitations imposed on them by others, Eights often work for themselves.

As employees, Eights can be huge assets or a lot of work, and they're usually both. If you're fortunate enough to have an Eight on your team and want her to perform well, keep the lines of communication open and don't surprise her by changing the rules or announcing a sudden change of plans. Eights are highly intuitive and read the world from their gut, so they can smell deception or a lack of integrity from a mile away. If they trust you, you've got it made. If they don't, sleep with one eye open.

Eights always want to know who has the power, so they will consistently challenge and test authority. So you have to set limits, provide regular, honest feedback, and establish clear and reasonable boundaries. Eights will follow a leader so long as it's clear the leader knows where they're heading. They have no patience for a leader who waffles or lacks the moxie to commit to a course of action and move. Because they're looking for a strong leader, you have to either cowboy up and provide them with clear direction or put someone in charge of them who has more gumption than you.

You also need to keep them active. A bored Eight is like a puppy who's been cooped up in the house all day: keep him busy or he'll gnaw everything in your house down to the studs. But when your back's against the wall, you want Eights on your team. They're creative, smart and fearless, they're terrific troubleshooters, and they'll sleep on the floor to make sure the job gets done.

Corporate America worships Eights. (Corporate America also prizes Threes, but we aren't there yet.) They're people like Jack Welch, the former chairman of GE, whose infamous candor and hard-hitting leadership style grew General Electric's bottom line exponentially but also earned him the nickname "Neutron Jack." (One has to wonder whether this gave him pause.) Regardless, Eights' commanding presence and boundless energy instills confidence in others, and people follow them.

As long as you're a man, that is.

FEMALE EIGHTS

Gender plays a role in how life unfolds for Eights. In the mid-1960s my father was unemployed and our family was broke—"newspapers in your loafers to keep your feet dry in the rain" kind of broke. To put bread on the table, my Eight mother took a secretarial job at a small publishing house in Greenwich, Connecticut. In those days old-boy networks dominated the publishing world, and to get ahead women didn't have to break through glass ceilings; they had to blast their way through steel-reinforced concrete walls. That didn't stop my mother. Fifteen years after she was hired to take dictation and make coffee, she was named vice president and publisher of her company.

That's an Eight: hard driving, tough, decisive, innovative, resourceful and accomplishing what people say can't be done. They just make things happen.

When she reflects on her

> "When men cut jobs, they're seen as decisive. When women do, they're vindictive."
> **CARLY FIORINA**

years in the business world, my mother will tell you that female Eights are the most misunderstood and unfairly treated number on the Enneagram. In our culture a male Eight is respected and revered. People lionize men who "kick ass and take names." Sadly, we all know the word people use to describe a woman in the workplace or the community who takes charge, stands up for what she believes, refuses to take crap from people and gets the job done.

I don't need to spell it out for you, right?

Many female Eights go through life scratching their heads and thinking, *Why do people experience and treat me this way?* Will the easily threatened and insecure please put a sock in their yaps and let these gifted women out of the penalty box so they can get on with their lives without further interruption?

WINGS

Remember, each basic personality type incorporates the attributes of at least one of the numbers on either side of it on the diagram. This is called your wing. If you're an Eight and you know which of your wings colors your type more than the other, you would say either "I'm an Eight with a Seven wing" or "I'm an Eight with a Nine wing." Or as my Scottish friends put it, "I'm an Eight with a wee bit of Seven in my blood."

We haven't learned about the hallmark traits of Sevens (the Enthusiasts) or Nines (the Peacemakers) yet, but that shouldn't stop you from seeing how each of these wings adds flavor and nuance to the personality of an Eight.

Eights with a Seven wing (8w7). This can be a wild combination. Eights with a Seven wing are outgoing, energetic and fun, reflecting the Seven's sunny personality. They are also ambitious, impulsive and sometimes reckless. These Eights live life to the fullest. They are the most energetic of all numbers and the most entrepreneurial. The Seven energy masks the more wary Eight so they are more social and more gregarious than other Eights.

Eights with a Nine wing (8w9). Eights with a Nine wing have a more measured approach to life. They are more approachable and more open to cooperation over competition, in keeping with the Nine's tendency to play a peacemaking role. Because of the Nine's gift for mediating, these are not ordinary Eights—8w9s can be conciliatory. They are supportive, modest and less blustery, and others are happy to follow their lead. When the Nine's gift of seeing both sides of everything is available to Eights, they become successful negotiators in situations both big and small.

STRESS AND SECURITY

Stress. When Eights get stressed out, they move to and take on those qualities you'd associate with unhealthy Fives (the Investigators). Here they withdraw and become even less connected to their emotions. Some experience insomnia and neglect to take care of themselves, eating poorly and not exercising. In this space Eights become secretive and hypervigilant about betrayal. They also may dig their heels in and become even more uncompromising than usual. That's something.

Security. Eights move to the healthy side of Two in security, where they become more caring and aren't so conscious of hiding their tender and gentle nature. Eights in this space don't insist their beliefs and opinions are absolutely right, but learn to listen and value other people's points of view as well. They start to trust in something bigger than themselves (yes, there are things in the universe larger than Eights) and allow others to take care of them—which, if even for a short time, makes everyone happy. Eights connected to the positive side of Two realize that justice is usually a reality beyond their control and that vengeance is something best left up to God. At least for now.

SPIRITUAL TRANSFORMATION

In his book *The Holy Longing*, Catholic writer Father Ronald Rolheiser describes *eros* as "an unquenchable fire, a restlessness, a longing, a disquiet, a hunger, a loneliness, a gnawing nostalgia, a wildness that cannot be tamed, a congenital all-embracing ache that lies at the center of human experience and is the ultimate force that drives everything else." Suzanne and I have a hunch that Eights are more in touch with, or perhaps even endowed with, a greater measure of this divine *eros* than the rest of us. They're finite creatures trying to manage an overfull tank of infinite desires. That's a lot to manage. When contained correctly, their fire can safely welcome and warm people. But like all fire, if not surrounded with a hearth of self-restraint, it will burn your house down.

When Eights are spiritually on the beam and self-aware, they are powerhouses: fearless, magnanimous, inspiring, energetic, supportive, loyal, self-confident, intuitive, committed and tolerant toward those who are weaker than they are.

When Eights switch their lives over to autopilot and spiritually fall asleep at the wheel of their personality, they become shamelessly excessive, reckless, arrogant, bull-headedly uncompromising and sometimes even cruel.

I'd love to help Eights tap into the childhood innocence they gave up too early and restore their trust in humanity. I'd like to promise them they won't be betrayed, but I can't. Eventually we all go under that knife.

The healing message Eights need to know, believe and feel is this: there are lots of trustworthy people in the world, and though the risk of betrayal is always real, love and connection will forever elude them unless they welcome and reconnect to the innocent, less defended child they once were. Yes, betrayal is exquisitely painful, but it doesn't happen as often as Eights fear it does. And if or when it does, they'll be strong enough to survive it.

Since Eights like people to be straightforward and direct with them I'm going to be brutally frank: living behind a façade of bluster and toughness to mask one's fear of emotional harm is cowardly, not courageous. Risking vulnerability and love is what takes courage. Are you strong enough to come out from behind the mask of boast and brusqueness? That's the real question.

I like Brené Brown's books *The Power of Vulnerability* and *The Gifts of Imperfection*. Actually, I suggest that Eights read each of them. Twice. In *The Gifts of Imperfection* Brown writes, "Embracing our vulnerabilities is risky but not nearly as dangerous as giving up on love and belonging and joy—the experiences that make us the most vulnerable. Only when we are brave enough to explore the darkness will we discover the infinite power of our light." Brown is on to something: vulnerability is the base metal of love and relationships. If Eights want to love and be loved they will have to risk opening their heart and revealing their innermost feelings to a trusted few. It's the price of admission.

"When I am weak, then I am strong." That's what St. Paul said, and I think he was right. Eights should write those words on a 3 x 5 card, tape it to their bathroom mirror, and make it their life's mantra. It will serve them better than "It's my way or the highway."

TEN PATHS TO TRANSFORMATION FOR EIGHTS

1. Too often, your intensity and lust for life runs the show. Give a friend permission to tell you when you're going overboard or exhibiting extreme behaviors. Remember, "Moderation, moderation, moderation."

2. To recover a piece of your natural childhood innocence, tend and befriend your inner child. I know, you don't have time for this sort of crap, but it helps.

3. Watch out for and avoid black-and-white thinking. Gray is an actual color.

4. Broaden your definition of strength and courage to include vulnerability. Risk sharing your heart at deeper levels with someone in your life.

5. Remember, your tendency is to act impulsively. It's "Ready, Aim, Fire!" not "Fire, Aim, Ready!"

6. You don't have a corner on the truth market. In the heat of battle, stop and ask yourself, *What if I'm wrong?* Say that a hundred times a day.

7. Your personality is twice as big and intense as you think it is, and what feels like passion to you often feels like intimidation to others. Offer an unqualified apology when people tell you that you ran over them.

8. Don't always play the part of the rebel, and try not to pit yourself against appropriate authority figures. They're not all bad people.

9. When you power up and get angry, stop and ask yourself whether you're trying to hide or deny a vulnerable feeling. What feeling is it? How do you use aggression as a way to hide it or defend against it?

10. Don't judge yourself or others as weak for sharing tender feelings. It takes courage to drop your guard and expose your inner child. (I know, you still hate that phrase.)

WHAT IT'S LIKE TO BE A NINE

1. I'll do almost anything to avoid conflict.

2. I'm not a self-starter.

3. Sometimes I get lost in doing trivial tasks, while things that really need to get done get put off.

4. I'm happy to go along with what others want to do.

5. I tend to procrastinate.

6. People seem to want me to be more decisive.

7. When I get distracted and go off task I give my attention to whatever is happening right in front of me.

8. I often choose the path of least resistance.

9. I find routines at work and home comforting, and I feel unsettled when something throws them off.

10. Others see me as more peaceful than I really am.

11. I have a hard time getting started, but once I do I really get things done.

12. I'm a "what you see is what you get" person.

13. I don't think of myself as being very important.

14. People think I'm a good listener even though I find it hard to pay attention in a long conversation.

15. I don't like to take work home with me.

16. Sometimes I tune out and think about the past.

17. I don't enjoy big social gatherings as much as a quiet evening at home with the ones I love.

18. Being outdoors is very soothing for me.

19. I am often quietly stubborn when people put demands on me.

20. It would feel selfish to spend a whole day doing whatever I want to do.

4

THE PEACEMAKER

You cannot find peace by avoiding life.

VIRGINIA WOOLF

Healthy Nines are natural mediators. They see and value the perspective of other people and can harmonize what seem to be irreconcilable points of view. They are unselfish, flexible and inclusive. These Nines are seldom attached to their own way of seeing and doing things. They've learned to make decisions based on the right priorities. They are inspiring, self-actualized people.

Average Nines, while they come off as sweet and easygoing, are stubborn and out of touch with their anger. These Nines overlook themselves. Though they generally feel unimportant, they occasionally wake up and realize they have to work on investing in themselves. They are willing to stand up for justice on behalf of others but would not likely risk doing much to stand up for themselves. They don't ask for much though they appreciate what others do for them.

Unhealthy Nines have trouble making decisions and become overly dependent. To dull feelings of sadness and anger they engage in numbing behaviors. Struggling to maintain the illusion that all is well, they can vacillate between acquiescence and open hostility.

In my early twenties I had a firsthand experience with someone who suffered from a sleep disorder. One night I was awakened by what sounded like the voice of a little child faintly singing downstairs in our kitchen. This was distressing. I had recently seen Wes Craven's film *Nightmare on Elm Street*, which featured a choir of creepy little kids who sang "One, Two, Freddy's Coming for You" every time he was about to carve up his next victim. Like Job, I felt "the terrors of the thick darkness."

Armed with a candlestick lamp, I snuck downstairs only to discover my sleepwalking housemate in the living room in his boxers mindlessly dancing in place while singing Madonna's "Like a Virgin." If we'd had smartphones back then I could have captured that moment, posted it on YouTube, and it would have gone viral—Gangnam style.

That memory still makes me laugh, but somnambulism, the medical term for sleepwalking, can actually be quite dangerous. Some people while sleepwalking have climbed 140-foot cranes, driven cars, walked out third-story windows and even murdered their in-laws. Heck, I think there are entire countries being run by people who are sleepwalking. But I digress.

Great Christian teachers have long used sleepwalking as a metaphor to describe the human spiritual condition. When our personalities are on autopilot they lull us into a half-sleeping state in which we find ourselves trapped in the same habitual, repetitive patterns of mindless reactivity we've been caught up in since childhood. It's predictable to the point of hypnotic. Nines suffer from a more aggressive form of somnambulism than other numbers. If they're not careful they can sleepwalk through life.

John Waters and Ronna Phifer-Ritchie are spot on when they say Nines are the "sweethearts of the Enneagram." My wife, Anne, and my daughter Maddie are both Nines. I adore them. When Nines are spiritually mature they are chill, easygoing people who know how to relax and go with the flow of life. Adaptable and even-tempered, they don't sweat the small stuff like so many of us do. They're Gore-Tex, not Velcro. The least controlling number on the Enneagram, Nines allow life to unfold naturally, and they offer others the freedom and space to grow in their own time and way. They are quick to love, slow to judge and rarely ask to be recognized for the effort they put into caring for other people. They're free and easy, down-to-earth, practical people who are eminently likable. Honestly, I can't say enough good about Nines who are doing or have done their work. But Nines are also no strangers to the principle of inertia. They know from experience that a body in motion stays in motion, and a body at rest stays at rest. When overwhelmed with too many things to do, too many decisions to make or the upsetting prospect of change, Nines can slow to a crawl. If they come to a full stop they know it might take a lot of energy to get themselves going again. As Suzanne likes to say, "Nines start off slow . . . and then they taper off." More about these foibles as we go.

THE NINE'S DEADLY SIN

The deadly sin of Nines is *sloth*, a word we usually associate with physical laziness. The sloth of Nines, however, is spiritual in nature. Average Nines are disconnected from the passion and motivational drive necessary to rise up and live their "one wild and precious life." Immature Nines don't fully connect to the fire in the belly they need to chase after their God-given life and, as a result, fail to become their own person. But tapping into those fiery passions and instinctual drives would upset the inner peace and equilibrium the Nine treasures above almost everything else. And now we're closer to the truth. For Nines, sloth has to do with their desire to not be overly bothered by life. They literally don't want life to get to them. Remember, Nines are in the Anger or Gut Triad. You can't lay claim to your life unless you have guts, unless you have access to your animating instinctual fire. But Nines are slothful when it comes to fully paying attention to their own lives, figuring out what *they* want in life, chasing their dreams, addressing their own needs, developing their own gifts and pursuing their calling. They cling to and protect their "Hakuna Matata" inner harmony. They ask little of life and hope life returns the favor. If Eights are too in touch with their gut instincts and overexpress their anger, Nines are out of touch with their gut and underexpress their anger. Nines are out of touch with the good side of anger, the part that inspires, drives change, moves things along and gives them courage to stand up for themselves. When you're unplugged from this side of anger, you become lethargic and dreamy.

This failure to risk fully engaging with life stems in part from the Nines' need to avoid conflict *at all costs.*

Nines fear that expressing their preferences or asserting their agenda will put important relationships at risk and upset the calm surface of their inner sea. What if their priorities and wants compete with the agenda of someone they care about and this difference leads to conflict and relational disconnection? What if asserting their own opinions, needs and desires creates disharmony between them and the people they love? Nines so value feeling comfortable and tranquil, maintaining the status quo, and preserving connections with others that they set aside their own viewpoints and aspirations to merge with those of others. This doesn't seem like a big deal for Peacemakers, who often grew up feeling like neither their presence nor priorities matter much to others. A Nine thinks, *Why rock the boat when*

FAMOUS NINES

Barack Obama
Bill Murray
Renée Zellweger

nothing I say or do ever seems to make much of a difference in the world anyway? Wouldn't it be easier and more comfortable not to assert my priorities and take the path of least resistance? As you can imagine there is often a hint of resignation in the air around Nines. Sadly, they pay a price for their "go along to get along" philosophy of life and not pursuing a life worthy of their gifts and spirit. They fall asleep to their lives.

To cope with having countless things to do and not knowing where to start, to avoid the backlog of unanswered questions and postponed decisions crying out for their attention, to keep their anger out of view, and to buoy a low self-esteem, Nines have unhealthy coping strategies. They will often turn to food, sex, drinking, exercise, shopping, the reassuring comfort of habits and routines, performing mindless busywork, or vegging out on the couch and watching TV to numb out and ignore their feelings, wants and desires. What Nines fail to realize is that numbing out is a bogus form of relaxation, a cheap imitation of the genuine peace for which they long.

But Nines should take heart: they are more courageous and resourceful than they know. Remember, on the Enneagram any number's blight is merely a distortion of that number's blessing. All of us have work to do. So, as Aslan the lion cries at the end of the Narnia Chronicles, "Further up and further in!"

ALL ABOUT NINES OR PEACEMAKERS

Nines share several common traits that characterize them as a group, like self-forgetting, difficulty making decisions and a tendency to be easily distracted. While not all Nines exhibit every single trait, many Nines will recognize themselves in what follows. (Or, at least, their friends and family members will immediately diagnose these traits in their beloved Nines, while the Nines will agree with what they say because maintaining harmony by agreeing with others is exactly how Nines operate.)

Self-forgetting and merging. Nines self-forget. All three numbers in the Anger Triad are self-forgetting. Eights forget rest and self-care, Ones forget to kick back and have fun more often, and Nines forget their opinions, preferences and priorities. Instead they merge with the feelings, viewpoints and pursuits of others and in so doing they erase themselves. To avoid kicking up a hornet's nest in their relationships, unevolved Nines neglect their soul's summons to identify, name and assert what they want in life and to go hard after it. In fact, they can merge so deeply with the life program and identity of another that they eventually mistake the other's feelings, opinions, successes and aspirations for their own.

Perched at the summit of the Enneagram, Nines enjoy an unobstructed view of the world. From this vantage point they not only have the benefit of seeing the world the way every other number sees it, but they also naturally incorporate into themselves a measure of the core characteristic strengths associated with every type. As Riso and Hudson observe, Nines can embody the idealism of Ones, the kindness of Twos, the attractiveness of Threes, the creativity of Fours, the intellectual horsepower of Fives, the loyalty of Sixes, the optimism and adventurousness of Sevens, and the strength of Eights. Unfortunately, from this privileged position Nines tend to see the world from the viewpoint of every number but their own. Or as Riso and Hudson put it, "The only type the Nine is not like is the Nine itself."

Because they can see through the eyes of every other number and are therefore unclear about who they are and what they want, Nines drop their healthy boundaries to fuse with a more assertive partner, whom they idealize and from whom they hope to glean a sense of identity and purpose. But after a while they don't know where they end and the other person begins. People will sometimes experience or describe Nines as blurry, passive, in "soft focus" or lacking a distinct self. Because they feel unimportant and as if they're not special enough to matter or change anything, Nines are conspicuously inconspicuous. Their diffuse energy can give others the impression that they're everywhere and nowhere at the same time. They can walk in and out of rooms barely being noticed. As Enneagram teacher Lynette Sheppard writes, "Being with a Nine can feel like falling into a big, comfortable space."

Average Nines have less stamina and energy than any other number on the Enneagram. They can take off like a rocket on a project, but then halfway into flight they succumb to inertia and "mission drift" and plummet back to the earth. There are often a lot of unfinished projects in a Nine's wake— half-caulked bathtubs, partially mown lawns, nearly organized garages. They

> "I have so much to do
> I'm going to bed."
>
> **SAVOYARD PROVERB**

may feel exhausted, and with good reason: Nines are smack in the middle of the Anger or Gut Triad. As you've learned, their neighbors the Challengers externalize their anger and—sorry for the spoiler— their other neighbors, the Ones, internalize it. To avoid conflict and inner turmoil, Nines fall asleep to their anger. This doesn't mean it disappears, only that they have to work hard to contain it and keep it out of their own view. This is a toilsome, soul-wearying enterprise.

Unlike Eights and Ones, Nines also have to erect and maintain not one but *two* boundaries—the first to defend their peaceful center from being negatively affected by the outer world, and the second to defend their serene interior against being unsettled by upsetting thoughts and feelings arising from within. It takes effort to ignore your anger and hold up two boundaries. It diverts energy that Nines could otherwise dedicate to more fully engaging with life and developing themselves. No wonder they feel inexplicably tired so much of the time. So tired that when they're not actively per- forming a task and they momentarily sit down to take a break, Nines will sometimes literally doze off.

Sometimes you'll spot a Nine staring detachedly into the middle distance as if they've checked out and fallen into a dreamy trancelike state. They have. When Nines feel overwhelmed—like when a conflict threatens to arise or people are telling them what to do—or sometimes for no discernible reason at all, they tune out and withdraw into a place in their mind that Enneagram teachers call the Nine's "inner sanctum." At these moments Nines uncouple from their anger and life energy and ignore the call to take action on something. Nines tell Suzanne and me that while in their inner sanctum they replay past events or conversations and what they wish they'd said or done differently. If anxiety is the cause of their retreat to the inner sanctum, they'll think, *Why am I upset right now? Is this my fault or someone else's?* Or at times they simply retreat to reconnect to or recover their comforting, albeit illusionary, sense of interior peace. If Nines fall too deeply into this hazy trance, they become increasingly absentminded and less productive, which only causes more problems for them in their relationships.

Because they sometimes lack drive and focus, average Nines often become jacks-of-all-trades but masters of none. They are generalists who, because they know a little bit about everything, can find something to talk about with everybody. Conversations with Nines are delightful as long as they don't switch over to cruise control. You'll know a Nine has done this when, after asking them how their day went, they launch into a long, drawn-out story containing more details and detours than you ever thought possible. It's this tendency to verbally meander at times that explains why some Enneagram teachers use the term *epic saga* to describe the Nine's talk style.

Ambivalence and decision making. Remember how each number on the Enneagram diagram is connected to two others by arrowed lines, indicating how the numbers dynamically interact with each other? Positioned at the top of the Enneagram, Nine has one foot in Three and the other in Six. Though we haven't covered either of those numbers yet, Threes are the most conformist or compliant of all the numbers while Sixes are the most nonconformist or anti-authoritarian of all the numbers. What this means for Nines is big-time ambivalence. Nines frequently feel torn between wanting to please others and wanting to defy them. When faced with having to take a stand or make a decision, Nines will smile and look calm on the outside, but inside they will feel overwhelmed by what to do: *Do I think this is a good idea or not? Do I want to do this or don't I? Do I say yes to this person's request or do I say no and risk disconnection?* To avoid disconnection, their conformist side will want to say yes to keep everyone happy, while their nonconformist side will feel like flipping them off for once again having to neuter their own feelings and desires to adapt.

Because there are so many angles from which to examine an issue, so many factors to take into consideration, and so many pros and cons to fret over, Nines often never get around to deciding. They sit on the fence and agonize over what to do while waiting for someone else to make the decision or for the situation to naturally work itself out on its own. All this fence sitting leads to procrastination, which can drive the rest of the world crazy. Though you may not pick up on it at first, the more you pressure a Nine to make a decision or do something the more they quietly dig their heels in and resist. Nines can and do make decisions, but given their ambivalent nature it can take them a long time. That there's a stockpile of unresolved questions and pending decisions already taking up real estate in their minds doesn't help speed the process along either.

If on a Friday afternoon I text Anne saying, "Where do you want to go for dinner tonight?" she will respond, "I don't know, where do you want to go?" This text always comes so quickly I'm convinced she has it preprogrammed into her phone. Remember, as a Nine Anne doesn't want to assert her preferences for fear they will create conflict or arouse unpleasant feelings between us. She wants to know what I want so she can adapt and merge with my desires, skirting potential disagreement. It's the telltale response of a Nine.

This exchange also reveals how hard it is for Nines to make choices when they're faced with unlimited possibilities. It's easier for Nines to know what they don't want than what they do want, so people who love a Nine would do well to offer them a limited set of options from which to select. If I send Anne a text saying, "Would you like to go out for Thai, Indian or Chinese tonight?" there will be a three-minute pause followed by a text saying, "Thai," with a thumbs-up emoji.

People who want to help a Nine should realize how important it is not to rob them of whatever choice they do make. I'm not as big a fan of Thai food as Anne is, so halfway to the restaurant I might think, *Anne probably doesn't care one way or another where we go for dinner, whereas I really want Chinese. If I tell her I want to go to Jolly Panda she'll happily agree.*

And I'm right, she will. But because I love Anne and I know she's working on the challenges of her Nine-ness, I want her decision to stand, and to let her lead. Nines already feel that their preferences and presence matter less than other people's. The last thing they need is for you and I to cosign that BS.

Let's look at one last aspect of Nines' ambivalence. Maybe because they're perched on the crown of the Enneagram where they can catch a glimpse of everyone's perspective, Nines can see all points of view. And they all seem equally valid. Their ability to see two sides to everything makes them natural mediators—and the kind of person everyone assumes is on their side. Suzanne's husband, Joe, a Methodist pastor, often sees couples for marriage counseling. Sometimes a woman in the congregation will sidle up to Suzanne at coffee hour on Sunday and whisper something like, "I'm so glad my husband and I are meeting with Joe. He understands where I'm coming from and who needs fixing in our marriage."

Fifteen minutes later the husband of the woman will take Suzanne aside and say, "I'm so grateful Joe's counseling us. Finally someone sees what I've been saying all along and knows I'm not crazy."

Picking up a pattern? Nines are so good at seeing and identifying with every viewpoint that people often walk away from them feeling the Nine not only understood them but also agreed with them, even though the Nine never actually came out and said so. Because they're so empathetic and able to recognize the merits of different perspectives, healthy Nines can often reconcile seemingly irreconcilable points of view. But this capacity to see both sides to everything can also create problems. Suzanne and I sometimes compare notes and laugh about the challenges of raising kids with people who see two sides to everything. When you catch your kids doing something wrong, do you send them to their room saying, "You just wait until your [insert other parent here] comes home and hears what you did"? Whenever Suzanne or I said that to our kids when they were growing up, they just nodded their heads and grinned slyly. They knew what would happen when that parent came home. First, Anne or Joe would listen to our side of the story and then go upstairs to talk to whichever of our kids was in trouble. Fifteen minutes later Joe or Anne would come back downstairs with the child peering out from behind them and say something like, "You know, the kid has a point." Understand that seeing and acknowledging both points of view is the average Nine's way of not having to take a stand and experience conflict or disconnection.

A task for growing Nines is to discern and declare which of two viewpoints is correct from *their* point of view.

> "Peace is the only battle worth raising."
>
> **ALBERT CAMUS**

Sadly, Nines will sometimes abandon their own opinion and defer to someone else's, either because they're uncertain or simply because they want to blend in and get along with them. Nines have to learn how to identify, give voice to and stick to their own point of view regardless of how much pressure they feel to change it in the moment to appease others.

A related challenge is the conundrum of prioritizing some tasks over others. Since all undertakings seem equally important to Nines, it's hard for them to decide what to tackle first. Every Monday morning when Suzanne's husband, Joe, walks into the office, his secretary hands him a list of what he needs to accomplish that week in order of importance. Joe is a supersmart guy who leads the oldest deeded church in Dallas. But without a list he'll just do the next thing that presents itself to him. Some Nines will resent it and go all subtly stubborn on you if you insist they start using a list, but without one they pose a threat to the civilian population at-large.

Although Nines seem to tread in ambivalence, there are times when they know exactly what they have to do and they do it, regardless of the controversy or conflict it will cause or how much it will cost them personally. At these moments Nines are acting on the basis of conviction. In the literature of the Enneagram this is called "right action."

We might be wrong, but Suzanne and I think Bill Clinton is a Nine. Between November 1995 and January 1996, President Clinton and then–Speaker of the House Newt Gingrich locked horns in an epic battle over cuts to the federal budget that resulted in two unprecedented shutdowns of the government. During the contentious, high-stakes negotiations between the White House and members of the Republican-controlled Congress, Clinton staffers worried the president would either acquiesce to Gingrich's demands or make so many compromises that he would irreparably hurt himself politically. Clinton hated conflict. At times he had trouble making and sticking to decisions, and more than once during his political career he had acquiesced to political rivals for the sake of making peace. But one night, after Gingrich had refused to accept the last of many deal offers, Clinton looked at him and said, "You know, Newt, I can't do what you want me to do. I don't believe it's right for the country. And it may cost me the election, but I can't do it." In the staring contest between Gingrich and Clinton over the government shutdown, Gingrich blinked first. A few days later Republicans agreed to reopen the government without a budget deal. Clinton won the next election. Many historians say making and sticking to that decision is what clinched Clinton's election to a second term.

White House staffers who were present when this exchange occurred say they knew they had witnessed something extraordinary take place inside Clinton. He exercised right action. Do you see how such action is the opposite of sloth? I have a feeling, though, that if Hillary asked Bill where he wanted to go to dinner to celebrate the outcome of his meeting with Newt, he probably would have shrugged and said, "I don't know, where do you want to go?"

Watershed moments of this magnitude will only present themselves a handful of times in a Nine's life, but as they work on themselves they can begin to take similarly bold actions in smaller matters. They can find the courage to initiate an uncomfortable conversation, go back to grad school to earn the degree and pursue the career they've always wanted, or refuse to bow to pressure from colleagues who want them to change position on a business matter.

Passive-aggression. Remember how I said when you first begin working with the Enneagram it can be painful? How all of us can feel exposed and ashamed when we discover the dark side of our type? This can be particularly true for Nines, who often overattach to and enjoy their reputation for being the good guy or the nice girl. If you're a Nine, keep in mind as you read the next few paragraphs that, as with every number, your curse is the flip side of your blessing; none of us are getting out of this book without feeling stung once or twice, and we're going to talk about what's beautiful about you before this is over. So . . .

People often ask Suzanne or me, "How can people who are so kind and friendly reside in the Anger Triad?" Despite their reputation for being sweet and accommodating, Nines aren't always sticking daisies into rifle barrels. Nines can be as angry as Eights, but you wouldn't know it given their affable and pleasant exterior. Nines are loaded with unresolved anger, but they're afraid the experience of letting it out will prove too overwhelming, so they fall asleep to it. Though they're out of touch with it, Nines harbor resentments going back to childhood or more recently for having sacrificed their own agenda or dreams to support yours or the kids'. Because they don't know when or how to say no to people, they feel angry that others seem to take advantage of their seeming inability to set boundaries in relationships. If that weren't enough, they feel annoyed when people tell them to wake up and start doing more than the minimum to get by. All this pressure upsets their inner calm!

Nines don't forget real or perceived slights, but because they're conflict avoidant they will rarely express their anger openly. Sure, every now and then Nines will blow their top, but most will maintain their almost Buddha-like calm and leak their ire indirectly.

If you do something to make a Nine angry on Monday morning, they often won't feel it until Tuesday afternoon. Come Tuesday night you'll know they have their hackles up with you over something when you ask whether they fulfilled their promise to pick up your dress from the dry cleaner for your important business trip tomorrow and in a nearly repentant tone of voice they

> "Trying to make her angry is like trying to find a corner on a bowling ball."
> **CRAIG McLAY**

say, "Oh dear, I forgot." Remember, for a Nine who lacks self-knowledge this is not necessarily conscious behavior. They're just humming along in the trance of their Nine-ness.

Stubbornness is the Nine's go-to passive-aggressive behavior, particularly when they feel like they're being pressured into agreeing to a plan or doing something they don't want to do. But they have other arrows in their quiver of passive-aggressive actions they can choose from when they want to indirectly express their anger over something or take control of a situation, such as avoidance, procrastination, stonewalling, tuning out, giving the silent treatment or not performing tasks that are clearly theirs to do, among other things. When a Nine's partner finally gets frustrated and demands, "Is something wrong?" the Nine might insist, "I don't know what you mean." Sadly, their passive-aggressive behaviors end up making others angrier, which only creates more conflict and problems for the Nine than if they'd just come out and said they were mad in the first place.

Because Anne knows I'm a stickler about being on time for things, she generally tries to be ready to leave, especially when it's really important for us to be punctual. From time to time, however, she pulls the equivalent of a longshoreman's union work slowdown. This forces me to stand at the bottom of the stairs looking at my watch and yelling for her to hurry up because we're going to miss the beginning of a movie or insult our dinner hosts.

Now that I'm familiar with how Nines operate, I know her slowing down to a snail's pace means that Anne's angry with me about something but doesn't want to spark an argument by telling me directly. She wants me to figure out why she's upset and fix the problem without her having to get involved. So now when this happens I go upstairs and say, "Okay, spit it out," to which she'll say, "Life was so much better before you knew the Enneagram."

Prioritizing and distractions. When faced with having to wake up and address their own priorities, Nines will sometimes focus on inessential tasks and leave the more essential ones until last. This is a baffling but effective defensive maneuver on the part of the Nine to turn their attention away from identifying their own life priorities, having to feel their anger and acting on their own behalf.

One Sunday afternoon I asked Anne, who teaches middle school history, whether she wanted to go to the gym, but she declined, saying her parent-teacher comments were due the next day and she hadn't started them yet. When I arrived home a few hours later I was surprised to find Anne polishing silverware. I didn't even know we owned silverware.

"What are you doing?" I asked.

"I found our wedding silver in the back of the corner hutch in the dining room and told Maddie she could have it. It was so tarnished I thought I'd polish it for her."

"What about your comments?" I asked. "Aren't they due tomorrow?"

"Fine," Anne said, abandoning the gravy boat. "I was just trying to do something helpful."

Nines are easily pulled away by distractions. Everyone else's priorities are more important than theirs, and such distractions are a great way to self-forget and avoid the pain of not knowing what you want in life. But wait—the human mind is marvelously creative—there's always more.

One night Anne and I invited my mom to join us for dinner at 6 p.m. At 3 p.m. Anne announced she was going to make a quick run to the grocery store to buy ingredients for the meal. At 5:00 she still hadn't returned, so I called her cell.

"Where are you? My mom's coming in sixty minutes. Have you been to the grocery store yet?"

Silence.

"Not yet. I was on my way there but Sue was out on her front lawn when I drove past her house so I stopped to say hello, and while we were talking

> "You know if we were sitting on the front porch talking and a horse walked by, my dad would just get on it and ride off."
>
> ***NATALIE GOLDBERG***

the chain on one of her kids' bikes fell off and she didn't know how to put it back on so I helped her. After I left I realized I had grease on my blouse so I stopped at CVS to buy some stain remover, and I remembered I had a prescription in my purse for Maddie's eye drops so I got that filled, and then when I was finally on my way to Whole Foods I drove past Bed, Bath, and Beyond and saw a banner up advertising a bedding sale, and Aidan will need new sheets and pillows for school in September, and I had a bunch of 20 percent off coupons in my purse so I ran inside and bought some, but now I'm almost to the grocery store and I'll be home in twenty minutes."

Do you see what happened? When a Nine gets sidetracked by a nonessential task or activity (e.g., stopping to chat with a friend), they can forget the Big Picture (e.g., in two hours Mama is coming for dinner). No longer seeing or feeling the urgency of the Big Picture, the Nine can no longer assign value to or prioritize tasks (e.g., buying food for hungry Mama *now*). Without said Big Picture (Mama ETA only sixty minutes), the Nine's attention loses focus and becomes diffused. Every task now seems to take on equal importance, so the Nine ends up doing whatever presents itself to them in the moment.

We all need friends or a partner who can ask us questions that wake us out of the trance of our particular number. "Are you still on task?" is a good question to pose to a Nine who appears to be busily doing everything and nothing at the same time.

NINES AS CHILDREN

I've never met a kid more easygoing, with a sweeter spirit and a preternatural talent for sensing the needs of others, than my daughter Maddie. Back when I was leading a start-up church Anne and I often entertained groups of people in our home. Four or five years old at the time, Maddie would walk into a room of adults and pick someone's lap to crawl into and curl up in a ball and fall asleep like a cat. When it came to making people feel peaceful, this kid was better than a Xanax and two glasses of wine. You could literally see a palpable wave of calm and relief fall over whomever Maddie picked to receive this special treatment.

One day a friend asked Anne, "Have you ever noticed when Maddie's looking around to decide whose lap she's going to curl up in that she always picks someone who's going through a divorce, a serious health issue or some other big life crisis?" We'd never made the connection before, but our friend was absolutely right. I think Maddie's gut told her who in the room most needed the peace and reassurance that everything was going to be okay. Her presence still communicates that today. Maddie lives in California and wants to be a therapist. She doesn't have her degree yet, but if I were you I'd make an appointment now. She's going to be busy.

Many, many Nines tell Suzanne and me they grew up in homes where they either were, or perceived themselves to be, overlooked and where their preferences, opinions or feelings were of less importance than those of others. The wounding message Nines heard is "Your wants, opinions, desires and presence don't matter much." My Maddie is not only a Nine but a middle child wedged between an older sister and younger brother who are both assertive numbers on the Enneagram. It saddens me, but I suspect Maddie sometimes felt like the classic lost child. I wish Anne and I had been familiar with the Enneagram when our kids were little. I would have known how important it was to make sure Maddie felt seen and important. Thankfully, she knows it now.

Nines as kids are very easy to be with. They're not always the first ones to jump into activities or shoot their hand up to answer a question in class, but they bring harmony and cheer wherever they go. As kids Nines feel very uncomfortable when there's conflict between parents and other family members, so they'll try to play the role of mediator while looking for a place to stand where they won't be forced to choose a side. If people are uncompromising and can't broker a peaceful solution, a child Nine may feel angry, but their anger is usually overlooked or ignored so they either keep it to themselves, mentally check out or hightail it out of the room. Often when my son Aidan and daughter Cailey got into a fight in the car, Maddie would put her head against the window and fall asleep to escape the conflict.

These little beauties feel like their ideas and feelings aren't valued, so they learn the art of merging very early in life. While they would prefer not being the center of attention for too much or too long, they long for us to notice and honor their presence. Like all kids they are looking for a place and a way to feel like they belong.

NINES IN RELATIONSHIPS

Mature Nines make wonderful partners, parents and friends. Loyal and kind, they will go above and beyond the call of duty to support you. They're fun, flexible and don't complain much. They love life's simple pleasures. If you give them the choice between getting dressed up and going to a black-tie gala or snuggling on the couch with you and the kids for pizza and a movie, they'll pick the latter. Nines always have their special place in the home where they can retreat to be quiet and engage in an activity that enhances their experience of peacefulness.

A healthy Nine is someone who has woken up and found their voice or come into their own. They know they're important enough to invest in and that they matter in the lives of their family, friends and coworkers. A healthy Nine is spiritually inspiring. They're receptive to the world, yet not so open or lacking in boundaries that they lose their sense of self-definition.

Nines who are asleep get in trouble in relationships when conflict arises (and when doesn't it?) and they refuse to acknowledge and resolve it. Denial is a big defense mechanism for them. They don't want to face anything that will unsettle their harmony, so they tell their inner orchestra to play louder while their ship is sinking. They might ignore the obvious signs that something's wrong, minimize the problems, or suggest a simple repair that only reveals how out of touch they are with the magnitude of the issue and how determined they are to avoid the unpleasantness of dealing with it. Because they want to avoid conflict and painful conversations, others have to hold Nines' feet to the fire to address serious problems in relationships. Their desire to skirt conflict and fuse with another person is so strong that Nines will cling to relationships long past their expiration dates.

Nines are not initiators, but they're thrilled when others reach out to them. They have a wonderful ability to reconnect with people whom they haven't run into in a long time. Even after years of not seeing a person, they can pick up the conversation as if it had only been yesterday when they last saw you.

Here's what I've learned being married to a Nine and parenting a Nine: what feels like a minor tiff to you feels like the Battle of the Bulge to them. What you hear as a fractional increase in the volume of your voice a Nine hears as yelling.

It's important that before I share my thoughts or feelings about something I ask Anne or Maddie what theirs are. This not only honors them, it lessens the possibility they will merge with mine and perhaps agree to do something they don't want to do.

NINES AT WORK

Position available for even-keeled, reliable, enthusiastic team player to work in harmonious environment. Approachable and diplomatic, this person must be able to get along with a wide range of people. Those who enjoy stirring up controversies or playing office politics need not apply.

If this want ad were to appear on LinkedIn there would be a mile-long queue of Nines clamoring to get an interview. It might even occasion an outbreak of violence among this usually peaceful population.

Healthy Nines are great workers and colleagues. Some have partners who believe in them and dedicate their lives to help them live into their potential (e.g., Nancy Reagan, Hillary Clinton). Supportive, nonjudgmental and inclusive, they build bridges and bring people together in a spirit of cooperation. Many Nines tell Suzanne and me they aren't particularly ambitious, though some are. They don't covet the corner office or need a big expense account. If they have a good job with reasonable pay and perks, they're content to stay where they are. Because they're able to see multiple points of view, Nines can solve problems and put together deals where everyone wins.

Nines draw their energy and derive a sense of identity from the group, so they would rather merge with the team and share the credit for a success than go out of their way to shine the spotlight on themselves to advance their career. They like a little recognition but mostly fly under the radar so as not to draw too much attention to themselves. What if their accomplishments at work lead to a change in duties or being assigned more work? When an opportunity for advancement comes up, Nines might pursue it—but only when they're ready. For the most part Nines aren't high-energy people, and they don't like feeling controlled or pressured to perform.

Creatures of habit, Nines appreciate structure, predictability and routine in the workplace. Nines don't like to bring work home, and they definitely don't like interruptions on weekends or vacation.

Nines make wonderful counselors, teachers, clergy and public relations executives. "Being a teacher is perfect for me," my wife Anne says. "I work best when I know there's a set pattern and rhythm to my life. I like knowing which classes I teach on what days, when semesters begin and end, when vacations are, and what the head of school expects of me. Most of all I have great relationships with my colleagues and I love the kids."

Unfortunately it's as easy to take advantage of Nines in the work place as it is in relationships. They're too accommodating. To avoid rocking the boat they say yes when they want to say no and often regret it later.

Nines tend to sell themselves short at work. They have considerable skills but undervalue them. Though capable of holding positions at the highest levels in the professional world, most Nines gravitate toward middle management where they can avoid the kind of conflicts and stress associated with leadership such as making unpopular decisions, supervising employees or having to fire people.

WINGS

Nines with an Eight wing (9w8). This is one of the most complex combinations on the Enneagram, given the Eight's need to go against power and the Nine's need to avoid conflict. Eights are energized by anger, while Nines avoid it at all costs. Talk about a walking contradiction! These two numbers bring a new twist to the "opposites attract" cliché, but it is also a powerful place within the

> "It's better to keep peace than to have to make peace."
> **UNKNOWN**

system. More energized, confident, stubborn, outgoing and inner-directed than the 9w1s, 9w8s have more access to anger and express it more openly if they or others are threatened. (Suzanne's daughter Jenny is a 9w8. She says, "Mom, I'm in so much trouble. My Eight wing just did a bunch of stuff it's going to take three weeks for my Nine wing to clean up.") Remember that this uptick in confidence and periodic aggression is relative to how other Nines behave, not to other numbers who have *way* more access to their anger and can express it more openly.

Though they will sometimes change their minds, 9w8s find it much easier to be clear and direct about things that are important to them. Although the Eight wing doesn't make it more likely that they will act on their own behalf, they are energetic in acting on behalf of the underdog and the common good. These Nines tend to be more confrontational than other Nines, but they are also quick to be conciliatory.

Nines with a One wing (9w1). Nines with a One wing (the Perfectionist) have a strong sense of the difference between right and wrong. One energy helps these Nines stay a little more focused, so they are able to accomplish more, which enhances their confidence. The 9w1s are more critical, orderly, introverted and passive-aggressive than other Nines. Because of their concern about matters of right and wrong they're apt to be involved in peacemaking efforts or other social justice causes. These Nines are principled and modest as leaders, and people want to follow them because of their integrity and steadfastness.

STRESS AND SECURITY

Stress. In stress Nines start to act like unhealthy Sixes (the Loyalists). They become overcommitted, worried, rigid, wary of others and anxious, even though they don't know why. These Nines become more self-doubting, which makes decision making even more difficult than usual. Interestingly, they also become reactive—a big departure for a number that is rarely, if ever, quick to react.

Security. When Nines are feeling comfortable and safe in the world they move to the positive side of Three (the Performer), where they are more goal-oriented, decisive, self-confident and in touch with their life's agenda. Flourishing Nines struggle less with inertia, take command of their lives and believe their presence in the world matters. More importantly, Nines connected to the positive side of Three can experience and enjoy *genuine* peace and harmony.

SPIRITUAL TRANSFORMATION

The Nine's weakness for merging is the dark side of an enviable spiritual gift. But in my mind the spiritual advantages of being a Nine more than make up for the work they have to do in their lives. If the goal of the spiritual life is the realization of union with God, then healthy Nines' ability to merge gives them a spiritual leg up on the rest of us. When it comes to attaining a unitive knowledge of God and becoming "one with Christ," healthy Nines almost always cross the finish line first. They're natural contemplatives.

Nines are open and receptive in every way. Even as kids, they seem to possess an innate awareness of the sacramental dimension of the world. They have a profound awareness of the interconnectedness of all things in creation. Lovers of the outdoors, they pick up on the presence of God in the natural world and how everything expresses God's glory. Because they value being over doing, Nines know how to rest in God's love and share themselves more generously than the rest of us. And because Nines are able to see both sides to everything, they're comfortable with paradox and mystery, which comes in handy when it comes to dealing with a religion that includes a virgin birth and a God who is both Three and One at the same time. If you're a Nine, be encouraged: when healthy, your capacity for merging can place you in the same league as other great Nine spiritual leaders like Pope Francis and the Dalai Lama.

But Nines resist the unsafe nature of real spiritual transformation. If you're a Peacemaker, your greatest motivation in life has been to avoid conflict and experience inner harmony, but what looks like peace is really just your desire to be unaffected by life. Spiritually, the absence of conflict is not the presence of peace, which requires work and risk. If nothing else, Nines should hear these words: Wake up and say yes to the adventure of *your own* life!

Nines are as important and as deserving of becoming their own person as everybody else is. It's their birthright. Waking up will involve reclaiming personal authority and responsibility for their life. It will mean finding and resurrecting *their own* thoughts, passions, opinions, dreams, ambitions and desires. This will be scary. They'll have to stop hiding and drafting behind other people. If Nines love themselves as much as they love other people, they will allow themselves to go on this adventure of becoming their own person. Paradoxically, the road to peace and harmony is littered with conflict and disharmony. Scrupulously avoid anything that promises a life of peace and tranquility without conflict or pain. Whatever it is will probably end you up in rehab.

Nines don't like to admit it, but they're angry. I get it. I'd be angry too if I repeatedly felt overlooked. They're angry for the sacrifices they've made to keep the peace and hold relationships together, but when they get the urge to stand up for themselves or act on their own behalf, they don't do it. Nines are afraid if they let their stored anger out it's going to hurt or kill someone, but that's not true. It might lead to conflict, which you can survive, but not homicide. Nines need to know that when they discover right action and move toward it, a feeling of self-worth will emerge in them. And others will notice and cheer them on as well. When this happens, they can stand and build on it so they don't have to slip away from themselves ever again.

The healing message Nines need to hear is "We see you and your life matters." God didn't invite you to this party to live someone else's life. We need *you* here!

TEN PATHS TO TRANSFORMATION FOR NINES

1. Journal on the question "What is my calling or life's program? Am I pursuing it or postponing it to keep the peace?"

2. Ask someone to help you find a task-management or to-do system to help you stay on task. There are lots of great apps out there just for this purpose.

3. Practice saying no when someone asks you to do something you don't want to.

4. Be aware of the numbing strategies you use to avoid having to deal with life, whether that's a glass of wine or shopping or Girl Scout cookies.

5. Don't be afraid to have opinions and express them. You can start with small things and build up to important ones.

6. Resist the urge to fall back on passive-aggressive behaviors like procrastination and avoidance. If you feel angry, be honest and open.

7. Understand how important and unique your voice is. People deserve to hear what you think, not have their own views mirrored back to them.

8. Remember that what feels like intense, terrible conflict to you might just be a typical disagreement for someone else. Take a breath and engage.

9. Realize that your tendency to merge with others can be a beautiful gift if directed toward God. Other types envy this spiritual advantage you have. But don't fuse with another person and miss out on the chance to become your own person.

10. When you feel paralyzed in the face of a decision, consult someone who won't tell you what to do but rather will help you tease out what *you* want to do—then do it!

WHAT IT'S LIKE TO BE A ONE

1. People have told me I can be overly critical and judgmental.

2. I beat myself up when I make mistakes.

3. I don't feel comfortable when I try to relax. There is too much to be done.

4. I don't like it when people ignore or break the rules, like when the person in the fast lane at the grocery store has more items than allowed.

5. Details are important to me.

6. I often find that I'm comparing myself to others.

7. If I say I'll do it, I'll do it.

8. It is hard for me to let go of resentment.

9. I think it is my responsibility to leave the world better than I found it.

10. I have a lot of self-discipline.

11. I try to be careful and thoughtful about how I spend money.

12. It seems to me that things are either right or wrong.

13. I spend a lot of time thinking about how I could be a better person.

14. Forgiveness is hard for me.

15. I notice immediately when things are wrong or out of place.

16. I worry a lot.

17. I am really disappointed when other people don't do their part.

18. I like routine and don't readily embrace change.

19. I do my best when working on a project, and I wish others would do the same, so I wouldn't have to redo their work.

20. I often feel like I try harder than others to do things correctly.

5

TYPE ONE

THE PERFECTIONIST

*Perfectionism is the voice of the oppressor,
the enemy of the people.*

ANNE LAMOTT

Healthy Ones are committed to a life of service and integrity. They are balanced and responsible and able to forgive themselves and others for being imperfect. They are principled but patient with the processes that *slowly* but surely make the world a better place.

Average Ones have judging and comparing minds that naturally spot errors and imperfections. They struggle to accept that imperfection is inevitable while fearing the tyranny of that critical voice in their head.

Unhealthy Ones fixate on small imperfections. These Ones are obsessed with micromanaging what they can. Asserting control over something or someone is their only relief.

When the teacher turned off the lights and turned on the projector I yawned, folded my arms to form a pillow on my desktop, and lay the side of my face down. As a seventh grader, I had no idea how Gregory

Peck's depiction of Atticus Finch, a widowed father and attorney tasked with defending a falsely accused black man in a small southern town in the 1930s, would silently plant a seed in my heart.

In *To Kill a Mockingbird* Atticus Finch wears a sensible, perfectly pressed seersucker suit with a pocket watch attached to a chain that he keeps in his vest pocket. He is the exemplar of a wise, measured and attentive father who treats his children with kindness and re- spect. He's an idealist, a reformer who feels a sacred duty to uphold the law and to make the world a more decent place for everyone. Imbued with a clear sense of right and wrong, he cannot turn a blind eye to injustice, and he isn't afraid to take a stand even if it costs him.

When his daughter Scout asks why he would bother defending his client Tom Robinson in a case he has no chance of winning and for which townspeople will revile him, Atticus tells her, "Before I can live with other folks I've got to live with myself. The one thing that doesn't abide by majority rule is a person's conscience."

Despite Atticus's brilliant and impassioned closing argument, Tom Robinson is found guilty by an all-white jury and led away. Downcast, Atticus packs up his briefcase and then slowly begins making his way down the aisle to exit the courtroom. As he does, those seated in the "colored balcony" stand one by one in a gesture of respect for him. When the elderly Reverend Sykes looks down and realizes Scout has neither noticed nor understood the symbolic gravity of the black community's getting to their feet to honor her father, he whispers down to her, "Miss Jean Louise? . . . Miss Jean Louise, stand up. Your father's passin.'"

That scene pierced me. Atticus Finch represented everything I wanted in a father but knew I'd never have as the son of a deeply troubled alcoholic. "With him, life was routine; without him, life was unbearable," Scout said about her father. I would have said the reverse about mine. Twenty years later, after my son was born, I came across an antique pocket watch that stirred my memory of

Atticus Finch. I bought it hoping that, when I looked at it, it would remind me of the kind of father I wanted to be.

That's the effect that Ones like Atticus can have on people. Sometimes their example inspires others to be better, to fight injustice, to embrace high ideals. But the One's commitment to living an exemplary life can quickly degenerate into a rigid perfectionism that can be tortuous both for Ones and for others.

THE ONE'S DEADLY SIN

Ones walk a thin line. When they're healthy, like Atticus, they inspire us with their concern for fairness and their desire to restore the world to wholeness. But when they tip toward average or unhealthy they can quickly get in their own way.

From the time they get up to the time they lie down, Ones perceive a world rife with errors and feel a bounden duty to correct it. There's no shortage of work to be done. Someone squeezed the toothpaste tube from the middle, the school secretary misspelled two words in the PTA newsletter, one of the kids didn't fold and hang their bath towel correctly, there's a fresh scratch on the car door, and the neighbors left for work leaving their trashcans at the foot of the driveway without the lids on.

> **FAMOUS ONES**
> Jerry Seinfeld
> Nelson Mandela
> Hillary Clinton

What kind of person does that sort of thing?

Ones need to be perfect. They chase perfection because they have this vague, unsettling feeling that if they make a mistake someone is going to jump out to blame, criticize or punish them. They compulsively strive to fix all that's broken in the world, but the work is never finished. *Irritated* doesn't begin to capture how this makes Ones feel at times. That others appear less concerned and interested in joining their crusade to put this world aright infuriates them even more. *Why don't people care as much as I do? Do I have to do everything myself? It's not fair.*

Anger is the deadly sin of Ones, but *resentment* is truer to their experience.

Ones believe the world judges people who don't follow the rules, control their emotions, behave appropriately and keep their basic animal instincts in check. For Ones, anger tops the list of feelings "good" people shouldn't express, so they bury the anger they feel about the imperfections they see in the environment, in others and in themselves. Ones are among the three numbers in the Anger Triad (8, 9, 1). Unlike Eights, who externalize their anger, or Nines, who fall asleep to it, Ones stuff their anger until it sits right below the surface, where it expresses itself to everyone as smoldering resentment.

But something else is fueling Ones' anger and indignation. Everywhere they look, people are having a grand old time indulging their desires or breaking the "rules" and not getting caught and punished for it, while Ones feel obligated to forgo doing what they want to do in order to do what they *should* do, namely, order our disordered world. To add insult to injury, they not only end up doing their share but they have to pick up the slack for all the jerks down at the beach drinking beer and playing volleyball when they have fun things they'd like to do as well.

Several years ago on *SNL* Dana Carvey played a character named Enid Strict, otherwise known as The Church Lady, who hosts a talk show called *Church Chat.* It's an over-the-top but iconic portrayal of One personality when it's in full bloom. If they're not careful, average Ones can adopt a similar Puritan-like attitude toward the world or, as Mark Twain put it, become "good in the worst sense of the word."

ALL ABOUT ONES OR PERFECTIONISTS

Walter is a tax attorney with a prestigious Wall Street accounting firm. When he comes home from work he likes the house to be clean, the kids to be bathed, dinner to be on the table and the world to be rightly ordered. I doubt Walter has ever come right out and told his wife Alice that these are his expectations, but it's not hard to pick it up in the air when Walter's around.

One night Walter comes home from work and the house is clean, the kids are bathed, and dinner is on the table. Now you'd think Walter would put his briefcase down and say something nice like, "Wow, this is awesome!" But the first thing Walter does is point at the couch and say, "The cushions are out of place."

Now, if I came home and said that to my wife Anne, she'd say, "Really? Let me show you where I can place those cushions."

In defense of Ones, that's just how they see. Wherever they go, errors and mistakes jump out at them and yell, "Fix me!" And they just can't leave it alone. They'll either say something or rearrange the cushions when you're not looking. What's important for us to learn as we study the Enneagram is that we can't change the way we see, only what we do with what we see. Walter has done a lot of work on himself since that unfortunate episode with Alice. If he did something like that today he'd immediately apologize. "I've got to keep working on that," he'd say, laughing. God bless Walter. The Enneagram has helped him come a long way.

Ones have high expectations of others and themselves. For average Ones, controlling their behavior and emotions is a priority. When an "uncivilized" impulse or unacceptable feeling arises, Ones will automatically push it down and bring up its opposite to negate it. In psychology this defense is called reaction formation. An example might be Ones who, when they hear your singing voice, will unconsciously stop their envy from rising to the level of conscious awareness and replace it with enthusiastic praise. At one level this is admirable, but because it is motivated by a self-interested need to not feel bad, the Ones' thin-lipped smile and kind words can feel forced.

Ones running on cruise control are mercilessly hard on themselves. Some demand perfection be maintained in only one corner of their lives (e.g., the yard, their boat, their office) while others apply it across the board. The house has to be immaculate, the bills paid on time. Thank-you notes need to be written and posted the same day gifts are received. Ones have to keep hard copies of tax returns for five years to avoid being in violation of IRS rules. Let's not even discuss the agony a poor One endures when they discover their credit score has dipped below 800.

They also impose their high standards on others. "Every Monday I would send our poor minister an email with a list of 'suggestions' to help her improve on what I didn't think worked at the previous morning's worship service," a now self-aware One shared at one of our Enneagram workshops. "I recommended better ways she could lead worship songs, tighten up her sermon, or shorten the Communion lines. I always ended with a reminder to begin the service at precisely 10 a.m. unless she wanted people to continue arriving late. Things are different now. My wife says she is proud of how I'm working toward being 'less helpful,'" he said, laughing.

If you suspect someone's a One but you're not sure, watch how they react when they open a dishwasher someone else has loaded. If they cluck their tongue and start reloading it while muttering something like, "Good night, why can't people do this correctly?" then there's a better than fifty-fifty chance they're a One. Sometimes a One won't let you finish stacking the dishwasher before they jump in to "help." They'll lean on the counter while you're loading it and say "eh-eh" when you place a mug where they think a bowl should go.

Most people can't endure being judged and harassed for too long by someone who has pinned a star to their shirt and elected themselves the kitchen sheriff. Eventually the harangued throw their hands in the air and storm out of the kitchen saying, "Is nothing ever good enough for you?"

I get it. As far as I'm concerned, if all the dishes fit and a little water hits most of them, who cares if they're perfectly arranged? What most people don't understand is that Ones don't think they're being critical. In their mind they're trying to help you! They think they're improving you! Doesn't everyone want to improve themselves like they do?

Not all Ones are fixated on flaws in the environment. Some Ones I know couldn't care less whether their house is a mess or when they see someone not picking up after their dog. Their need to be good and improve things expresses itself through their concern and commitment to addressing social ills. The activist and legendary consumer protector Ralph Nader is a One. You don't want to mess with that dude or any One who gets involved with efforts to put an end to wrongs like sex trafficking, corrupt politicians or companies polluting the environment. One of the reason Ones are attracted to supporting righteous causes is because it's not only okay but *appropriate* to openly express anger about injustice without feeling like you're being a bad girl or boy.

Because they believe they occupy the superior moral, ethical and spiritual high ground, Ones believe their way is the only right way of seeing and doing things and therefore feel justified in being judgmental and critical of others. They're usually not trying to come off that way, though. "People tell me my voice and body language come off as shaming and judgmental even when I'm consciously trying to sound kind," my friend Janet says. That the One's talk style is *preaching* doesn't help. No one likes to feel like someone is talking down to them.

All of us have a reproachful voice that gets triggered from time to time when we do something stupid and then goes away. As a rule Ones have a merciless inner critic; unlike ours, *it never goes away.* It's punishing. It's relentless. *Why do you always put your foot in your mouth? What kind of parent forgets to pack his kid's lunch in her school bag? How do you expect to make a sale when you can't even tie a proper knot in your tie? Get down and give me fifty!*

Heck, sometimes a One's inner critic will blame them for screwing up things they weren't even involved with or responsible for. After years of programming it's hard for Ones to shut off that cruel voice.

Ones caught in the trance of their personality believe not only that their belittling inner critic speaks ex cathedra but that it actually has their best interests at heart. *How would I have progressed this far in life without that voice harshly reminding me of what I was doing wrong or to prevent me from lowering my standards? If it weren't for my inner critic always pointing out my deficiencies, how would I know how to live beyond reproach? Think of how many more mistakes I would have made without it!*

Ones are terrified of making a mistake. Ones work themselves way too hard, and because there's so much to get done they don't often relax or let themselves have fun. As a result, they become pressure cookers whose regulator valves can't keep up with the buildup of resentment they feel toward the imperfections they see everywhere; the resentment they harbor toward themselves and others for failing to adhere to their high standards and for not helping out; and their outsized fear of making mistakes or acting inappropriately. It's quite a surprise when a normally very controlled and tightly buttoned-up One blows a valve. When it happens someone almost always gets burned.

> "What is this self inside us, this silent observer, Severe and speechless critic, who can terrorize us?"
>
> *T. S. ELIOT*

No matter how you look at it, the One's crusade to perfect the world is a fool's errand. There's always an unmade bed in it somewhere. Until they begin a spiritual journey they'll never know a minute's peace.

Given the stream of negative self-commentary their inner critic levels at them all day, Ones don't receive criticism well. Would you express gratitude to a fellow writer who pointed out your failure to insert a comma after an introductory phrase if the finger-wagging carper living in your head had already been comparing your grammar to fetid effluvium from the moment you started work at 3:00 a.m.? Please, people, one mugging at a time.

Though very sensitive to criticism themselves, Ones are shocked when you tell them you feel like they're being harshly critical of you. Seriously? You're only being given a thimble-sized sample of the bitter self-recrimination they drink from every day.

Ones can be critical and judgmental of other people. The unaware One will criticize people for failing to live up to their standard of perfection and also because misery loves company. It brings Ones a sense of relief if they can catch and criticize someone else for doing something incorrectly or behaving improperly because it levels the playing field: *Thank goodness! Someone besides me is deficient.* Of course, taking pleasure in someone else's shortcomings is a kooky way to tie the score, but it beats feeling like you're the only one who ever makes mistakes on the field. That's a lonely position.

Ones get the job done. So those are some of the challenges that come with Ones. But can you imagine a world without them? If it weren't for Steve Jobs's uncompromising passion for creating flawlessly designed products, there would be no Apple. If it weren't for high-minded leaders like Mahatma Gandhi and Nelson Mandela who couldn't abide injustice, India and South Africa might still be under the oppressive yoke of European colonialism. If it weren't for spiritual teachers like Richard Rohr, we wouldn't have as clear a picture of the loving heart of God.

Since Ones live in a world riddled with mistakes, they keep a running list of things that need doing. Some are so thoughtful and generous that they make lists of things for you to do as well. Come Saturday morning the spouse of a One can expect to find a honey-do list on the kitchen counter long enough to keep them busy for an entire summer and into deer-hunting season.

Many Ones value etiquette (for example, think of Martha Stewart) and know how to host a great dinner party. Their homes are normally spotless and thoughtfully decorated. Because they want you to have a perfect time, they'll cook a beautiful meal and they'll be prepared to introduce great topics for table conversation. Recently someone told me that while sitting vigil at his mother's deathbed she repeatedly asked him if the house was tidy and if he was using the good china to serve coffee to the family members who were gathered downstairs awaiting news of her passing. Talk about a good host.

Ones want to be good people. They always want to do the right thing. How would you react if you were sitting in a bus station when a mentally ill person walked in and announced, "I'm homeless, I haven't eaten for days, and I need help"? Regardless of what anyone else would do or what they themselves would want to do, Ones would believe it was *their* responsibility to make sure the person received proper care. Why? That's the correct, responsible and right thing to do. We should all expect this of ourselves.

Ones believe that every task should be done in a systematic and correct fashion. When they read the directions to assemble a recently purchased grill—and those directions say not to do anything until you make sure you have all the necessary parts—Ones actually set out all the screws, nuts and bolts and count them. Then they double-check.

If by chance one of the four plastic cups that fit on the end of each leg is missing, Ones will say to their spouse, "We can't put this thing together tonight. We're short one piece."

Now, if the spouse is a Nine he or she might say, "Don't worry about it; we can get a pack of matches and put it under that leg to keep the grill level."

True Ones will respond firmly, "Not on my watch," and then will call the 800 number to ask for the missing black cap to be shipped ASAP so every step will have been followed correctly. The reason

Ones won't settle for a jerry-rigged grill is they know that every time they look at it the only thing they'll see is that one missing black leg cap. (Ones break out in hives at our house. We've got packs of matches keeping the place level on the foundation.)

ONES AS CHILDREN

Growing up, Ones try to be model kids. They know the rules and follow them to the letter. They spend lots of energy com-

> "Have no fear of perfection—you'll never reach it."
>
> *SALVADOR DALI*

paring themselves to other kids, so a conversation during the ride home from school will include a little bit about themselves, but it will mostly be about comparing themselves to other children and their successes, failures and mishaps. Think of eleven-year-old Hermione Granger getting on the train to Hogwarts and immediately comparing notes about what spells the other kids could do and whether they had read *Hogwarts: A History.* This comparing and judging mind remains with Ones their entire lives.

That inner critic makes its presence known early, so Ones are hard on themselves. They sometimes shy away from sports or other group activities where they may not excel, since perfection is the goal at a very early age. They ask lots of questions about whether they're doing things right, and they take responsibility for things that aren't their fault. It's hard for children to figure out right from wrong, but these kids sure try.

While Ones aren't great multitaskers (it's hard to do more than one thing perfectly at a time), they don't usually mind when they are asked to pick up toys, straighten their bed or tie their shoes. Neatness and order are comforting to Ones even when they're small. It makes them feel safe and less anxious.

Have you seen or read Marie Kondo's book *The Life-Changing Magic of Tidying Up*? Whoa. Starting when the professional organizer was five years old, she would browse longingly through magazines showing perfect meals and lovely interior design. So she started re-organizing her family's belongings at home and the teacher's things at school, skipping recess in order to rearrange the bookshelves in her classroom. All the while she would complain about the school's poor storage methods. "If only there was an S-hook, it would be so much easier to use," she would sigh. I'll bet you dinner at my favorite rib house in Nashville that Marie Kondo is a One.

Listen, it's hard being a perfectionist. So hard, in fact, that someone wrote and published an children's book titled *Nobody's Perfect: A Story for Children About Perfectionism* to help these little people before their inner critic permanently sets up shop in their heads. The wounding message little Ones pick up is that they have to be "good" and do things "right." Mistakes are unacceptable. People and things are either perfect or wrong. Period.

One kids need to be told that making mistakes is normal, that they can be imperfect and loved at the same time. They can develop into the healthy side of One more naturally if they are given the healing message that mistakes are just part of the process of learning and growing up. If you're parenting a One, make sure you correct them when no one else is around so as not to shame them in front of others. These kids may seem confident all the time, but they are more thin-skinned than you might think.

ONES IN RELATIONSHIPS

To form intimate relationships or deep friendships, Ones first have to overcome the difficulty they have making themselves vulnerable to others. Author Brené Brown calls perfectionism a "20-ton shield" we use to defend ourselves against being hurt. Unfortunately, what perfectionism really does is defend us against connecting with others.

For Ones, putting down the shield will require relinquishing their need to keep their emotions tightly buttoned up all the time.

They'll also need to acknowledge their fear of making mistakes, their sensitivity to criticism, and their concern about saying or doing the wrong things. It takes a lot of courage for Ones to be this transparent, but they can do it.

I once heard Helen Palmer say something to the effect that Ones don't throw a lot of hugs around or gush "I love you" every five minutes, but that doesn't mean they don't. Ones say I love you by being responsible and doing what's expected of them to make the world a better, more secure place for you. They will make sure you always get your annual physical. They'll make life work on a budget, and every meal they cook for you will be the right portion size, and contain the right combination of proteins, fats and carbohydrates.

What, you wanted more hugs? Remember how, after that hurricane, yours was the only house in the neighborhood with power and heat because years earlier your One dad bought a backup generator and regularly checked to make sure it was properly serviced and fueled? Sounds like a hug to me.

ONES AT WORK

No one cares more about details than Ones, so there are certain career paths we want them to pursue.

I flew from Los Angeles to Sydney, Australia, last year on an Airbus A380, the largest plane in the world. I'm usually not a nervous flyer, but the size of this plane spooked me. How could something so huge possibly get off the ground, let alone stay in the air for sixteen hours?

Prior to departure the co-captain took a stroll through the cabin welcoming passengers aboard, and he happened to notice I had a book about the Enneagram on my lap.

"My wife's into the Enneagram," he said, pointing at the book. "She says I'm a One, whatever that means."

"It means I have nothing to be nervous about," I said, breathing a sigh of relief.

Because they believe that tasks should be carried out methodically and that it's important to follow procedures and protocols, you not only want Ones to pilot your plane, you also want them to be the engineer who designs the brake system on your car, the pharmacist who fills your prescriptions, the programmer writing the code for your company's new website, the architect drawing up plans for your dream house, the accountant preparing your taxes and the editor combing through your latest book. And though I pray you never need one, you for sure want your cardiologist or neurosurgeon to be a One as well. Ones make top-notch lawyers, judges, politicians, military personnel, law enforcement officers and, of course, teachers.

Industrious, reliable and well organized, Ones thrive in structured environments where they know what the deadlines are and who is responsible for what tasks. Because they're afraid of making mistakes, Ones need regular feedback and encouragement. They so appreciate clear guidelines they might take the 800-page HR manual home on the first day at their new job and read it from cover to cover. They won't argue when they're docked a day's wages for showing up late to a job site so long as everyone else who showed up late receives the same penalty.

Ones are great at sizing up what's not working inside a company or organization and devising new systems and procedures to get it running right again. A major state university hired a One friend of mine to overhaul its health and benefits department. In three years she transformed it from the most poorly run office on campus into a department that was so efficient other universities sent their benefits people to model their own departments after its example.

But there can also be problems with Ones in the workplace, like their tendency to procrastinate. It's not a good sign if you spy a One tapping the eraser end of a pencil on her knee while staring blankly into a dark computer screen. Though they're self-disciplined and driven to succeed, some Ones can put off starting or completing a project for fear they won't do it perfectly. The occasional bout of procrastination, compounded by their hesitation to make quick decisions for fear of making a mistake, can slow things down for a whole team. This same fear of making mistakes will lead Ones to check and recheck their work forever, so others might have to encourage them to let it go and move on to the next task.

Ones typically have trouble adapting to change, resent being interrupted when working on a project and globalize problems; they think if one part of the business is tanking, then the whole business is going under. If they discover a flaw in a business plan, they worry the whole plan is flawed and might need a major or complete overhaul.

Because they're afraid of criticism or failure Ones will quickly disavow responsibility when something goes wrong. It's not unusual to hear a One say, "It wasn't my fault" or "Don't blame me; I didn't do it."

As leaders, Ones work hard to support people who work for them, particularly those who demonstrate a real desire to improve. At times, however, Ones can be controlling, rigid and stingy with praise even when it's deserved. They also can have difficulty delegating because of concern that a task won't be done correctly unless they do it themselves. Some Ones will annoy their coworkers to no end by redoing all sorts of tasks they think others have failed to do right the first time. Ones who extend their barrage of self-criticism to their colleagues are not generally the most popular people at the water cooler.

Finally, Ones at work—just like Ones in other areas of life— struggle with naming and owning their anger. If you work with a One, you need to know that when they start ranting with a disproportionate amount of angry energy about something, like the jerk who took their parking space, that's probably not what they're angry about. Their anger is about a tiff they had with their spouse that morning that they've worked hard to stuff and not acknowledge all

day, and now it's leaking out sideways. If you listen, gently ask clari-
fying questions and give them enough space, Ones will eventually be
able to trace a line back to what it is that actually made them angry.
They need a little help to figure out what's really going on with them.

But here's one of the things I love about Ones. When healthy they
are deeply committed to helping others become their absolute best.
They no longer seek to perfect the other person but to help them
self-actualize without shaming or scolding. My friend Melanie, an
Episcopal priest and mature One, says, "In all the work I have done,
I have always enjoyed every opportunity I have had to build people
up by affirming their hard work and talents. This is one of the
greatest gifts in my ministry. Jesus calls us to share in God's mission.
Paul calls us to share in building up the church. As a minister this
invites me into the delight and joy of encouraging people to bring
their best to God and to work with people to discern what gifts of
the spirit God has given him for the realization of the kingdom." I
can't tell you how helpful it would have been if I'd had a spiritually
well-put-together One mentor me when I was a young man.

That said, if you want someone who is efficient, ethical, metic-
ulous, reliable and does the work of two people, then hire a One!

WINGS

Ones with a Two wing (1w2). Ones with a Two wing are more extroverted, warm, helpful and empathetic on the high side of Two, but
they can be more critical and controlling on the low side of Two.
They are effective in problem solving for both individuals and
groups. They are generous in their response to church, education,
community, government and family. Ones with a Two wing talk too
much and try to accomplish too many tasks in a day.

Ones with a Two wing tend to have a more rapid pace of speech,
and because of it they quickly transition from teaching to preaching.
Under the influence of Two, Ones will more readily sense other

people's needs. Unlike Twos, however, they don't feel an irrepressible urge to meet those needs.

Ones with a Nine wing (1w9). Ones with a Nine wing tend to be more introverted, detached and relaxed. More idealistic and objective, they are often more circumspect, thinking before they speak to avoid saying something wrong or erroneous. They will pause before finishing a thought. Ones with a Nine wing are outwardly more calm and mull over decisions for a long time—this wing exacerbates rather than helps the One with procrastination.

The laid-back, easygoing stance of 1w9s helps in building and maintaining relationships. Without the influence of the Nine, Ones tend to have too many expectations for others, so when they feel let down, the result is often resentment.

> "The thing that is really hard and really amazing is giving up on being perfect and beginning the work of becoming yourself."
>
> ***ANNA QUINDLEN***

STRESS AND SECURITY

Stress. In stress Ones instinctively take on the not-so-great qualities we'd expect to see in unhealthy Fours (the Individualists). Their inner critic begins working overtime, and their need to perfect the world goes into overdrive. They become more resentful of others having fun, more sensitive to criticism, and depressed. In this space they long to be free of obligations and responsibilities, lose confidence, and feel unlovable.

Security. In security Ones take on the great qualities we associate with healthy Sevens (the Enthusiasts), where they're more self-accepting, spontaneous, fun, open to trying new things and being both/and rather than either/or. Here the voice of their inner critic gets quieter, they're not as hard on themselves, and they shift their attention from what's wrong about the world to what's good and right about it. This move to Seven in security often happens when Ones are away from home and feel less responsible for improving or fixing things. Ones can become entirely different people when they go somewhere for a week of fun in the sun.

SPIRITUAL TRANSFORMATION

If you're a One, you believe the only way you'll know peace on the inside is if you perfect everything on the outside. It's not true. That tranquility only comes when you surrender your compulsive need for perfection and stop stifling your emotions, particularly your anger. Don't hide your true self behind that veneer of perceived perfection. *A person does not need to be perfect to be good.* That's worth repeating several times a day until it gets deep down into your marrow.

> "And now that you don't have to be perfect, you can be good."
>
> **JOHN STEINBECK**

Ones' journey toward wholeness will have to include befriending their inner critic. As our One friend Richard Rohr says, "What you resist, persists"—which in this case means that Ones shouldn't bother telling their inner critic to shut up as it only gives it more power. Many Ones say it helps to give the critic a funny name so when it goes on the attack they can say something to it like, "Cruella, thanks for helping me navigate the world as a kid, but as an adult I don't need your help anymore." Or Ones might simply laugh and tell Nurse Ratched to turn down the volume.

Ones do well to remember there's more than one right way of doing things. Serenity means live and let live. Life isn't always either-or, black or white, right or left. Brené Brown sums up the healing message Ones need to hear: "You're imperfect, and you're wired for struggle, but you are worthy of love and belonging." It's so often quoted it's threadbare, but I can't resist mentioning the chorus to Leonard Cohen's song "Anthem"; it was written for Ones:

Ring the bells that still can ring
Forget your perfect offering

There is a crack in everything
That's how the light gets in.

TEN PATHS TO TRANSFORMATION FOR ONES

1. To awaken self-compassion, try to capture in a journal the typical things your inner critic says to you and then read them aloud.

2. When your inner critic activates, smile and tell it you hear it and appreciate how it's trying to help you improve or avoid making mistakes, but you're taking a new path to self-acceptance in life.

3. Resist the urge to give other people to-do lists or to redo their tasks if you think they haven't met your standards. Instead, catch the people you love doing things right—and tell them how much you appreciate them for it.

4. When you are ready to dive right in to correct an injustice or right a wrong, first ask yourself whether the passion you feel for that issue is really misplaced anger about something else.

5. Let your Seven and Nine friends help you learn how to relax and have fun. The work will still be there tomorrow.

6. If you find yourself procrastinating, think about the reason why. Are you reluctant to get going on a task or project because you're afraid you won't be able to accomplish it perfectly?

7. Pick up a hobby you enjoy but are not especially good at doing— and just do it for the love of it.

8. Forgive yourself and others for mistakes. Everyone makes them.

9. See whether you can catch yourself measuring yourself against others to see who does a better job, works harder or meets your definition of success.

10. Be aware of how you receive criticism from others, and try to accept it without being defensive.

WHAT IT'S LIKE TO BE A TWO

1. When it comes to taking care of others, I don't know how or when to say no.

2. I am a great listener, and I remember the stories that make up people's lives.

3. I am anxious to overcome misunderstandings in a relationship.

4. I feel drawn to influential or powerful people.

5. People think I'm psychic because I usually know what other people need or want.

6. Even people I don't know well share deep stuff about their lives with me.

7. It seems like people who love me should already know what I need.

8. I need to be acknowledged and appreciated for my contributions.

9. I'm more comfortable giving than receiving.

10. I like my home to feel like a safe and welcoming place for family and others.

11. I care a great deal about what people think of me.

12. I want other people to think I love everyone, even though I don't.

13. I like it when the people who love me do something unexpected for me.

14. Lots of people ask me for help, and it makes me feel valuable.

15. When people ask me what I need, I have no idea how to answer.

16. When I'm tired I often feel like people take me for granted.

17. People say my emotions can feel over-the-top.

18. I feel angry and conflicted when my needs conflict with others'.

19. Sometimes it is hard for me to watch movies because I find it almost unbearable to see people suffer.

20. I worry a lot about being forgiven when I make mistakes.

6

TYPE TWO

THE HELPER

I want you to be happy,
but I want to be the reason.

UNKNOWN

Healthy Twos can often name their own needs and feelings without fear of losing relationships. They are generous in their efforts to love well and care for others. These happy, secure Twos also have appropriate boundaries, knowing what is theirs to do and what is not. They create a comfortable, safe space for others and are often considered to be a friend to many. Loving and lovable, they adapt well to changing circumstances and are aware of the true self that exists beyond their relationships.

Average Twos are convinced that the expression of their own needs and feelings will automatically threaten the stability of their relationships. They are generous people, but they often consciously or subconsciously expect something in return for their efforts. They have poor boundaries and generally only know themselves in relation to other people. They are attracted to powerful people, whom they expect to define them, and they'll use flattery to pull them in.

Unhealthy Twos are codependent. In their desire to be loved they will accept almost any substitute: appreciation, neediness, companionship and purely utilitarian relationships. These Twos are insecure, manipulative and often play the role of the martyr. They don't give so much as invest, trying to earn love by meeting others' needs—but always expecting a high return on that investment.

After seminary I accepted a job at a congregational church in Greenwich, Connecticut. To get to know the community I went to a luncheon for local clergy where I met Jim, a Baptist minister from a neighboring town. Both Jim and I were young, new dads and secretly beginning to wonder whether deciding to go into ministry was like deciding to get a tattoo when you're drunk—something we should have thought through a little more carefully. Desperate for support, Jim and I agreed to meet once a month for breakfast at a diner to debrief the previous day's worship services and talk about the victories and vicissitudes of serving churches. We became fast friends.

One Monday Jim and I pulled into the parking lot of the diner for our standing breakfast appointment at the same time. To my surprise he was driving a brand-new Chevy Suburban. I chuckled as I watched him try to finesse it into a space. It was more like watching someone dock a Carnival cruise ship than park a car.

"That's a nice ride for an associate pastor," I said to Jim as he climbed out and hit the lock button on his key fob. "Did you get a raise?"

"It's a long story," he sighed, shaking his head.

"I can't wait to hear it," I said, holding open the diner door for him.

Over coffee and Greek omelets Jim told me how he and his wife Karen became "proud" owners of a Suburban. The story involved a successful middle-aged realtor named Gloria who was a beloved and active member of his congregation. Chatty, warm and unconscionably cheerful, Gloria knew how to make everyone feel like they were her best friend. She hosted a popular Bible study for high school girls, who she encouraged to stop by her home or call at any hour if they needed a shoulder to cry on. She volunteered for everything from teaching Vacation Bible School to coaching the local softball team.

A few weeks earlier Jim had been driving his twin girls to preschool in his old Nissan Sentra when Gloria pulled up in the lane adjacent to him at a red light. When she realized Jim was in the car next to hers she honked and waved at him, made funny faces and blew kisses at the girls. When the light turned green Jim waved goodbye to Gloria and drove off. As he did he glanced in his side view mirror and caught a glimpse of Gloria eyeing his car with the kind of expression one normally reserves for looking at a box of abandoned puppies.

To be fair, Gloria had reason to be concerned about the structural integrity of Jim's car. Jim's ten-year-old Sentra was a testimony to the power of duct tape and prayer. The car's body was dented and dinged from bumper to bumper, and the muffler, affixed to the car's undercarriage with a coat hanger, roared like the engine of an F-15.

The following Sunday, Jim and his family arrived home from church to find Gloria in their driveway. She was clapping her hands and bouncing on her toes like a sugar-jacked college cheerleader next to a brand-new Chevy Suburban with a giant red bow on the hood. Jim and Karen wondered whether they were at the right house or had taken a wrong turn and accidentally driven onto the set of *The Price Is Right*. They were still unbuckling their seat belts when Gloria rushed at them, jabbering so fast it sounded like she was speaking in tongues. She hugged Jim when he got out of the car and told him he was the best associate pastor the church had ever had. Wiping away tears, she ran to the other side of the car, threw her arms around Karen, and gushed on and on about how she was the model of a pastor's wife.

Soon the twins were out of their car seats and dancing around the new Suburban like Israelites around the golden calf while Gloria explained how seeing Jim at the stoplight in his old Sentra had broken her heart and made her anxious for his family's safety. She just knew they needed a new car but probably couldn't afford to buy one on a pastor's salary, so she felt moved to buy one for them.

Jim and Karen were speechless; something about this transaction gave them the "uh-oh" feeling. They tried to find words both to express their gratitude and to voice their concern about accepting such an extravagant gift, but Gloria wouldn't take no for an answer.

"Jim, I'm blessed to be a blessing," she said, pressing the keys to the new car into his palm.

"I know Gloria meant well," Jim said to me. "But that car's cursed. The rest of the pastors at church are grumbling because no one's ever given them a car. Karen won't drive it because she can't see over the steering wheel, and it eats more gas than an aircraft carrier."

"Can't you tell Gloria it's not working out and return it?" I said.

Jim shook his head. "Are you kidding? Every time I see her she asks if we still love the Suburban and if she can do anything else to help us."

I've got a strong hunch Gloria is a Two on the Enneagram.

THE TWO'S DEADLY SIN

Twos are some of the most caring, kind, supportive, upbeat and tenderhearted people on God's green earth. Three of my closest friends are Twos (one of which is my coauthor, Suzanne), and together they radiate enough love and generosity of spirit to heat a metroplex. Twos are the first responders in a crisis and the last to leave a dinner party if there are still dishes to wash. In Enneagram-speak they're called the Helpers.

If you suspect you might be a Two, then sit down, grab a box of Kleenex, light a scented candle, and take a few deep breaths before you read the next few paragraphs. Of all the numbers on the Enneagram, Twos are the most sensitive to criticism, so you'll have to take my word for it when I say this ends well.

Twos, Threes and Fours compose the Feeling or Heart Triad and represent the most emotion-oriented, relationship-centered and image-conscious numbers on the Enneagram. All three of these types believe they can't be loved for who they are, so each projects a false image they believe will win the approval of others.

FAMOUS TWOS

Mother Teresa
Archbishop Desmond Tutu
Princess Diana

Twos need to be needed. They rely on other people needing them to bolster their fluctuating self-worth. Presenting a cheerful, likable image and helping others is their strategy for earning love. For Twos, words of appreciation border on the intoxicating. Expressions of gratitude like "What would I do without you?" or "You're a lifesaver!" make a Two feel good—I'm talking "Justin Bieber just retweeted me" good.

Pride is the deadly sin of the Two, which sounds nonsensical because Twos appear to be more selfless than self-inflated. But pride lingers in the shadows of Twos' hearts. It reveals itself in the way they focus all their attention and energy on meeting the needs of others while at the same time giving the impression they have no needs of their own. The sin of pride comes into play in the way Twos believe other people are more needy than they are and that they alone know best what others require. They relish in the myth of their own indispensability.

Twos are indiscriminate caregivers. They foist their assistance and advice on those they deem to be weaker, less experienced and less capable of managing their lives than they are—people who would otherwise be lost without them. It's hard not to pat yourself on the back when you have an almost supernatural gift for detecting what others need and a seemingly unlimited supply of time, energy, treasure and talent to rescue them. Twos love to jump on their white horse to save the day when others require their assistance, but they can't imagine asking someone to lend them a hand when the situation is reversed. Twos rarely ask for help, at least not directly, and they don't know how to receive it when it's offered. It makes sense to Twos that others have to rely on them, but for them to rely on others? Never in a million years. Not to put too fine a point on it, but Twos suffer from an inflated view of their own power, independence and value to others. What lies beneath that pride? Terror. Twos fear that acknowledging their wants will end in humiliation and that *directly* asking someone to fulfill their needs will lead to rejection. *What if the person refuses me?* they ask. *How would I survive the shame and humiliation? It would only confirm what I've known all along: I'm unworthy of love.*

Though they're not always conscious of it, the help unevolved Twos provide others comes with strings attached. They want something in return: love, appreciation, attention, and the unspoken promise of future emotional and material support. Their giving is calculated and manipulative. Twos think if they can wrest appreciation and approval, and evoke a feeling of indebtedness in others, then others will sense when they require help and provide for their needs without their having to ask for it. Unconsciously they're drawing up a kind of quid pro quo arrangement: "I'll be there for you as long as you promise to be there for me without my having to acknowledge or ask you for help."

Twos believe they live in a world in which you have to be needed before you can be loved, and where you have to give to get. And because they don't believe you'd keep them around if they ever failed to render you service, Twos find it hard to put a cap on the time and energy they'll devote to taking care of you. It's a wonder to behold when you see an immature Two behind the wheel of the Love Train. Once it leaves the station it's all but impossible to stop it.

ALL ABOUT TWOS OR HELPERS

Twos have an amazing way of making other people feel safe and comfortable. The moment you walk into my pal Suzanne's home you feel like you've landed on an island of calm in a crazy world. It's filled with giant cushioned chairs, bowls of mini Godiva chocolates, votive candles, sacred art hanging on the walls, and Henri Nouwen and Mary Oliver books thoughtfully placed on side tables for guests to read at their leisure. It feels like a cross between the Ritz-Carlton and a Catholic retreat center. Twos accept you just as you are; they aren't judgmental, and they create a space both physically and emotionally in which people can speak from their hearts and experience.

On the other hand, as Richard Rohr says, "Twos are always on the make." That's because Twos live in a tit-for-tat world. Whether through charm, flattery, crafting a likable image or bald-faced people-pleasing, Twos are always trying to seduce or entice people because they don't believe others will be there for them when they need it unless they keep up this cheerful and fawning exterior.

Average Twos are unaware that there are unstated expectations and ulterior motives behind their helping behaviors. They see the acts of service they perform for us as generous and unselfish, not based on the unspoken assumption we will reciprocate. They don't wake up in the morning and say to themselves, *Gee, my friend Janet is swamped at work. To earn her expressions of approval and affection, and to ensure that she's there for me when I need her, I'm going to leave a casserole and a bag of Hershey's Kisses on her doorstep.* It's not until the following week when the tables are turned and the now-overworked Two is seething with resentment because neither Janet nor any of the other ingrates she's helped in the past brought her a casserole that the Two's true motives are revealed. When Twos get healthy, however, they can recognize what's happening and compassionately say to themselves, "Oh no, I did it again. I expected that to come back in kind and it didn't! I need to keep working on that."

When Twos walk into a room full of people, their attention immediately goes to "How are you doing? What do you need? What are you feeling?" and, most importantly, "What do you want?" They are so attuned and responsive to other people's pain you'd sometimes think they're psychic. This is an example of how what's best about your number is also what's worst about your number. It's great to have the gift of being attuned to other people's needs and helping them. But it's *never* good when a Two or any other number leverages their superpower to manipulate people to give them what they want.

Because their self-worth depends on the response they receive from others, Twos always end up giving away too much power to other people. When my Two friend Michael was first married, he wanted to express his appreciation to his wife, Amy, for working two jobs to keep them financially afloat while he was in grad school. So while she was still at the office Michael cleaned the house, set up a card table with candles and a pot of her favorite herbal tea, and stuck Post-Its all over the house with love messages written on them. Distracted and tired when she arrived home, Amy (who is *not* a Two) walked right past the table without noticing it. A full two hours went by before she saw it and said, "Are those flowers for me?" By then it was too late. Michael had already worked up a head of steam and was oozing resentment. He had spent hours putting together this surprise, and his miserable wife hadn't even noticed. The night ended with their having an enormous fight over Amy's lack of appreciation *for Michael.* "The next day I realized I hadn't just wanted Amy's appreciation. I had wanted her to fall at my feet and venerate me as though I were the patron saint of selfless giving. Later in our marriage I realized how my self-esteem was tied to the way Amy and others responded to my being a Helper. That's a lot of power to give away."

Twos are always on the lookout for signs of whether other people appreciate them. My friend Reynolds, a Two, is a brilliant author and speaker. He once told me that for him, public speaking is a nightmare. "I would always lock in on the crowd's response," he said. "Whenever I was in front of a group of people I felt like I had a 3-by-5 card taped to my forehead with the words 'Do you love me yet?' written on it. Inevitably my helper antennae would pick up the negative signals emanating from the one vaguely unhappy-looking audience member, and I would do everything but stand on my head to please them. When nothing I did elicited that all-important look of approval and appreciation, I would leave feeling like a failure."

Twos are afraid people will ditch them once they can stand on their own two feet. Suzanne is the mother of four great kids who adore her. From the day they were born she has enjoyed a close relationship with all of them, but for the longest time she was sure they wouldn't want to hang out with her once they were grown and married. She had always thought, *Once they're done needing me, they'll be gone.* What Twos don't know is that people don't have to need them every second of the day to still want them in their lives.

> "Act without expectation."
> *LAO-TZU*

Twos can walk into a party and intuit which couple had a fight on the way over, who would rather be home watching baseball and which person is anxious about losing her job. They can sense what other people are feeling without asking for a show of hands. The talk style of the Two is *help and advice.* So much as hint that you need something and an immature Two will chime in with "helpful" suggestions (or their plan to help you). The problem is that not everybody at the party wants a Helper getting all up in their business. Twos have to learn how to practice discernment. Before they leap into action like a Labrador retriever galumphing into the ocean to rescue a drowning child, they have to ask themselves, *Is this mine to do?* If someone is actually drowning, dive in to help him. Otherwise, opt for restraint.

Average Twos tell Suzanne and me they have the ability to sense and then fulfill the needs of others. The key word here is *sense.* You don't have to tell Twos what you require; they just know. The problem is they assume everyone has the same ability to sense other people's inner life as well. This can lead to arguments that begin with someone throwing his hands up in the air and saying, "I'm not a mind reader. How was I supposed to know what you wanted?" and end with the Two storming out of a room yelling over her shoulder, "I'm tired of having to tell you what I need when you should just know!"

For a Two, feeling out of gas is frightening because their self-worth relies on the continual supply of gratitude and appreciation they get from others for taking care of them. If they're spent, they won't be able to give, and then what use are they? At this point a burnt-out Two might have an outburst because they feel taken for granted. When it happens it's like watching a satellite burning on re-entry into the atmosphere.

Suzanne is a consummate Two. As a speaker and a pastor's wife, she gets lots of opportunities to be a Helper—maybe too many. This is what it sounds like when she comes home feeling fed up and fried and walks into the kitchen, where Joe is cleaning up.

"How are you?" Joe asks.

"Done."

"Done with what?"

"Everything. Nobody appreciates me. People count on me to give, give, give, and they don't even thank me. Now everyone's doing wonderfully and I'm spent. In fact, everyone I do things for is feeling so great right now I bet they're probably having a party and forgot to invite me." For the next few hours Suzanne will slam doors, hand Joe her church membership resignation because the leaders of the church have not once thanked her for teaching thousands of Sunday school classes, or threaten to get their kids on a conference call to ask why they never *once* expressed their gratitude for all the years she woke up early to press their school clothes. At their best, Twos are warm and generous, and at their worst they're resentful martyrs.

TWOS AS CHILDREN

Kids who compulsively want to please *everyone* are probably Twos. As kids Twos are usually sociable and have close friendships, but because they're worried that no one is going to want them they will try to buy or maintain love by giving away a favorite toy or their lunch.

Unusually sensitive, these kids wear their hearts on their sleeves. Sometime there's a hint of sadness about them because they don't see themselves as lovable. Once they learn that being helpful can earn a smile and praise they'll be the first to volunteer to help their soccer coach put away the equipment after practice or to ask their teacher whether they would like them to pass out supplies. In time these kids can adopt the role of the people-pleaser and overestimate its value to the overall operating of the family, school or sports team. As children, they can be independent early on because they see their own needs as problems to avoid.

Somewhere these kids picked up the wounding message that having or expressing their own needs will lead to humiliation and rejection. They're aware of everyone's feelings and try to adapt their behavior and image to what others want. Never assume that just because Two children know *your* needs that they also know their own. If a Two hits a rough patch and you ask them what they need, they'll most likely say they don't know. Press them and they might become frustrated or emotional. Twos spend so much time and energy focusing on the needs of others that they lose touch with their own. By the time they reach adulthood that is the pattern of their lives.

TWOS IN RELATIONSHIPS

If you're fortunate enough to have a Two in your life then you know relationships mean everything to them. I mean *everything*. Of all the numbers on the Enneagram, Twos are the most interpersonal. Warm and tactile, they easily move toward other people. For example, Suzanne can't walk past someone she knows without touching them on the arm, patting them on the back, or stopping to take their face into her hands so she can look them in the eye and say something like, "Now, you know I love you, right?"

But it's important for Twos to know we love them as well.

They feel things deeply, and it's easy for them to express emotions. What you might not know is that most of the feelings Twos have are not their own. Twos feel what *you're* feeling. It doesn't take long for the children of a Two to figure out that Mom or Dad feels their feelings more than their own. But once they do, it's like they're playing poker with house money.

All three of the numbers in the Heart or Feeling Triad are hunting for a sense of personal identity. One way Twos attempt to establish identity is by identifying and seeing themselves through the lens of their relationships. So rather than introducing themselves by their own name, they focus on their relationship to people you might know. It's always, "Hi, I'm Amy's husband" or "I'm Jack's mother." Twos need to learn how to individuate, to become their own person.

For Twos, this journey often begins in midlife when, after years of putting everyone else's needs ahead of their own, they become exhausted. One day they wake up and realize, *I can't go on giving this much. I need to take better care of myself.* This is a difficult but necessary passage for Twos, as well as for the people who have grown accustomed to the way they put others first and pressure them to go back to the good old days when the unaware Two put everyone else's interests ahead of their own. When the time comes, it's important for others to encourage Twos to become their own people who care for themselves appropriately.

TWOS AT WORK

In professional life, Twos often play second in command, but this doesn't feel demeaning to them. They know sergeants run armies, not generals, so they're more than happy to be the power behind the throne. When I was in elementary school, the principal's secretary was a kind, energetic and warmhearted woman named Miss Parker. Miss Parker sat in the main office, where she answered the endless stream of phone calls, calmed overcaffeinated irate mothers, let us take fistfuls of M&M's from a bowl on her desk when we received good test grades, made sure the students with peanut allergies brought their EpiPens to school, encouraged frazzled teachers, and at 3:00 put on an orange vest and monitored after-school pickup. If you needed love, lunch money or an emergency organ transplant at my elementary school, you went to Miss Parker. I'm sure the principal was a good guy, but I don't even remember his name.

Twos are intuitive people with highly developed interpersonal skills who need to work in positions where there's a lot of people contact. Twos build community. They know who's doing well around the office and who isn't. They remember people's birthdays and the names of everyone's kids. First to get the inside scoop, they know the backstory to everyone's divorce, whose kid needs rehab, and who's pregnant before anyone else does (even the father). As leaders they know how to recruit the right people to accomplish a task and use encouragement and praise to inspire and motivate them. They're empathic, optimistic, and—because they're image conscious—they know how to make an organization shine in the eyes of the outside world.

> "The catch about not looking a gift horse in the mouth is that it may be a Trojan horse."
>
> **DAVID SELLER**

Supervisors need to have the freedom to provide constructive feedback when their employees need it. People who supervise Twos, however, should keep in mind that too much criticism or harsh words will crush them. Twos aren't as interested as other types in climbing the ladder—or if they are, they keep their desire for recognition and attention outside their awareness because admitting they want it makes them vulnerable to disappointment.

Contrary to popular belief, there are plenty of male Twos in the world. After thirty-five years of working on Wall Street, my friend Jamie founded an organization and yearly conference that brings promising young leaders together with older accomplished leaders in the hope that they will form friendships and mentor one another. His Two personality shows itself in his passion for connecting people with one another and coaching younger folks on the ways they can avoid the pitfalls commonly associated with early career success.

WINGS

Twos with a One wing (2w1). Twos with a One wing (2w1) are concerned about doing things properly. They want to be seen as dependable and responsible. With a One wing these Helpers are more critical of themselves, more controlling and more prone to guilt. These Twos have clearer boundaries and are more aware of their emotional needs but have more trouble expressing them. They are less trusting and expect a bit more in return for their efforts.

Twos with a Three wing (2w3). Twos with a Three wing (2w3) are more ambitious, image-conscious and competitive. Extroverted and sometimes seductive like the Three (the Performer), they are more concerned about relationships and connections than Twos with a One wing. These Twos are more confident, so they achieve more; being seen as successful is a close second to being known as loving and generous. In this space Twos with a strong self-image can shape-shift like Threes to become whatever is called for to achieve the desired results.

STRESS AND SECURITY

Stress. Twos in stress take on the characteristic behaviors of an unhealthy Eight, where they become demanding and controlling, either directly or manipulatively. They blame other people for what makes them unhappy and can be surprisingly aggressive and vengeful about past wrongs.

Security. When they're feeling secure Twos move to the healthy side of Four, where they're okay with not having to pretend they love everybody. These Twos have some understanding of the need for self-care and can focus inward, where they invest in themselves by doing creative things, which brings them joy. This is the place Twos can imagine feeling good about themselves when they aren't helping someone else.

SPIRITUAL TRANSFORMATION

As is the case with every number, what's great about Twos is what's not so great about Twos. When people give too much, help for the wrong reasons, or serve others for selfish reasons rather than because they're called by God, their giving becomes calculating, controlling and manipulative. If you're a Helper, this chapter has likely been a difficult read for you.

Twos have long been afraid that people will reject them once they discover the Twos have needs and unattended sorrows of their own. Twos live in service to the lie that the only way to win love is through hiding the screwed-up, vulnerable people they really are behind the appearance and activity of a cheerful, selfless helper. Like all numbers in the Feeling Triad, they believe that if they show their true selves to the world, it will lead to rejection. The healing message for Twos is "You're wanted." Twos' needs matter, and they can begin now to learn how to directly express their real feelings and desires without undue fear of humiliation or rejection.

All Twos have to learn the difference between self-interested and altruistic giving. Self-interested giving expects payback, whereas altruistic giving comes without any strings attached. As the saying goes, "When you give and expect a return, that's an investment. When you give and don't expect anything back, that's love."

Thankfully, with a little self-knowledge and self-awareness, Twos can learn to give to others free of charge. If you're a Two that means you give exactly what's yours to give—nothing more and nothing less. If your friend Isabelle is buried at work and you babysit her kids but she doesn't reciprocate when you're in a similar crisis, then it won't matter to you because you had no expectation she would. As my twelve-step sponsor reminds me, "Expectations are resentments waiting to happen."

Think back to my friend Jim from the beginning of this chapter. He didn't want, need or ask for Gloria's help. In fact, her "help" turned out to be anything but. How differently that story would have ended if a more self-aware version of Gloria had gone to Jim and said something like, "Jim, the other day at the stoplight I noticed your car looked like it might be on its last legs. For some reason God has given me more money than I need, and I'd be happy to sit down with you and Karen to see if there's a way I can help. No pressure, just let me know if you need a hand."

It's a hackneyed story, but Twos might find it helpful to read the story of Martha and Mary in Luke 10. The account begins with the words "As Jesus and his disciples were on their way, he came to a village where a woman named Martha opened her home to him" (v. 38). Isn't it interesting that it was both Martha and Mary's home but only Martha gets credit for inviting Jesus and the disciples to come visit them? Was Mary inhospitable? Or of the two sisters was it only Martha who felt compelled to meet the needs of Jesus and the disciples?

When Jesus and his friends arrive, Martha does what any good Two would do, which is set to work making sure everyone is comfortable and has what they need. She has probably already washed Jesus' feet, and now she's running around to the point of distraction making dinner while her good-for-nothing sister Mary is chilling at Jesus' feet. Martha starts feeling jealous and resentful. Everyone else is in the living room throwing back olives and laughing while she's working her butt off in the kitchen cooking a lamb.

Martha gets angry because *as usual* she is doing all the heavy lifting and says to Jesus, "Are you just going to let her sit here while I do all the work? Tell her to help me." I'm not sure, but I think this is the only place in the Bible where someone actually orders God to do something. Like I said, hell hath no fury like an overworked Two who is feeling unappreciated.

Jesus knows what's really going on and replies, "Martha, Martha, you are worried and upset about many things, but few things are needed—or indeed only one. Mary has chosen what is better, and it will not be taken away from her" (vv. 41-42).

For Twos the lesson is simple: sometimes you think you are serving God or other people when you're actually not. Sometimes all the doing and caretaking is not what God is calling you to do. The Bible never tells us that Martha *asked* Jesus what he wanted; she took it on herself to make a big to-do. Maybe God simply wants Twos—and all of us—to relax in his presence.

If Twos are going to learn how to attend to their own needs as much as they pay attention to the needs of other people, they have to work on their soul in solitude. If they try to do this work in community they'll be tempted to help those around them grow spiritually rather than focus on their own development. In this situation Twos' tendency to drop everything to help people in crisis is more a defense against facing their own needs and feelings than an act of service. In their time with God they might ask themselves, *Who am I when no one needs me?*

TEN PATHS TO TRANSFORMATION FOR TWOS

1. Rather than hinting at your needs or leaving it to others to figure them out, try telling them directly.

2. Internally take a deep breath and start over when you catch yourself trying too hard to present a likable image or flattering others to win their approval.

3. Don't reflexively say yes to everything. When someone asks for your help, say you'll get back to them with an answer once you've had time to think about it. Or just experiment with saying the word *no*. It's a complete sentence.

4. When the urge to rescue or help overwhelms you, ask yourself, *Is this mine to do?* If you're not sure, talk it over with a trusted friend.

5. When you realize you've fallen back into the typical behaviors of your number, gently ask yourself, *What would I have to feel if I wasn't flattering or meeting this person's needs right now?*

6. Whenever possible, perform acts of anonymous service.

7. Twos toggle back and forth between having overly inflated and overly deflated views of themselves and their value to others. Remind yourself you're neither the best nor the worst. Just you.

8. Don't push away feelings of resentment or entitlement when they arise. Instead, view them as invitations to look inwardly with kindness and ask, *What most needs attention in my life right now?*

9. Don't beat yourself up when you catch yourself moving too aggressively toward others or overwhelming them with your emotions. Congratulate yourself for spotting it, and dial it back.

10. Two or three times a day, ask yourself, *What am I feeling right now?* and *What do I need right now?* Don't worry if you can't supply an answer. It takes time to develop self-care muscles.

WHAT IT'S LIKE TO BE A THREE

1. It's important for me to come across as a winner.

2. I love walking in a room and knowing I'm making a great first impression on the crowd.

3. I could persuade Bill Gates to buy a Mac.

4. The keys to my happiness are efficiency, productivity and being acknowledged as the best.

5. I don't like it when people slow me down.

6. I know how to airbrush failure so it looks like success.

7. I'd rather lead than follow any day.

8. I am competitive to a fault.

9. I can find a way to win over and connect with just about anyone.

10. I'm a world-champion multitasker.

11. I keep a close watch on how people are responding to me in the moment.

12. It's hard for me to not take work along on vacation.

13. It's hard for me to name or access my feelings.

14. I'm not one to talk much about my personal life.

15. Sometimes I feel like a phony.

16. I love setting and accomplishing measurable goals.

17. I like other people to know about my accomplishments.

18. I like to be seen in the company of successful people.

19. I don't mind cutting corners if it gets the job done more efficiently.

20. People say I don't know how or when to stop working.

7

The Performer

The real question is, can you love the real me? . . .
Not that image you had of me, but who I really am.

CHRISTINE FEEHAN

Healthy Threes have transcended the goal of merely looking good and are moving toward being known and loved for who they are, not for what they accomplish. They still love to set goals, rise to challenges and solve problems, but their self-worth is not tied to these things. They try to balance their abundant energy between work, rest and some kind of contemplative practice, recognizing the importance of *being* instead of *doing*. They feel valuable, which unleashes a tender benevolence that is focused on the common good.

Average Threes push achieving to overachieving, spending too much time at work or the gym. Highly driven, their need to perform even extends to the time they spend coaching the children's soccer team or volunteering at church. They see love as something to be earned, so they quiet their inner convictions, valuing what others define as success and striving to do more and do it better. They are confident in their abilities but also image conscious, constantly worrying that a poor performance will cause them to lose standing in other people's eyes.

Unhealthy Threes find failure unacceptable, which renders them unable to admit mistakes and causes them to behave as though they are superior to others. Desperate for attention, these Threes may turn the deadly sin of self-deceit into the sin of intentional deceit, telling others fabricated stories about themselves and their accomplishments in order to maintain their image. At their worst, unhealthy Threes can be petty, mean and vengeful.

I grew up in Greenwich, Connecticut, home to many of the most successful hedge fund managers, venture capitalists and investment bankers in the world. There are more Threes who live in Greenwich than child actors in rehab. Chief among them was my father.

Like all Threes, my father believed he could only be loved by being or appearing to be successful, avoiding failure at all costs and matching his image to please a crowd. For a number of years he had a glamorous, high-visibility career in film and television as managing director of Columbia Screen Gems Motion Pictures in Europe and the Middle East until at age forty he lost everything through a series of terrible personal and professional decisions. In regard to his career my dad was a failure, but you'd never have known it from looking at him or listening to him.

Even when our family was financially on the ropes my father continued buying handmade suits from Jermyn Street in London, drove a pricey (albeit secondhand) British sports car and managed to be the only person I know who could pull off wearing a cravat. He'd tell people stories about how Mel Brooks and Carl Reiner performed comedy sketches in our living room when we lived in London; about going on safaris with William Holden; and how the actor Roger

Moore, who played James Bond, had my father to thank for his career. Every story was "true" but embellished, and he made it sound like they'd all happened in the last month, not a decade earlier.

My dad believed well-heeled Greenwich folks only really value people who are accomplished, wealthy, sophisticated and well connected, so he morphed into "that guy" to win their admiration.

But my dad's talent for projecting the perfect image to impress a crowd wasn't limited to high-society Greenwich types. He could do it anywhere with anyone. Here's how it worked: when my dad arrived at a party the first thing he did was read the room. He wanted to know the general makeup of the crowd—who was there, what their preferences, values and expectations were—as if trying to answer the questions, *What persona do I need to craft and put on to win these people's approval? Who do they want me to become before they'll love and admire me?* Once he knew the answer to those questions (which took all of thirty seconds), he performed an instant makeover and became "that guy." Seriously, I once witnessed my dad walk into a group of car mechanics standing around a service station garage, and before you could say "carburetor" he'd picked up on their mannerisms, talk style, mood and general demeanor. My dad didn't know the difference between a muffler and a glove compartment, but by the time we left, those mechanics thought he could've been the host of NPR's *Car Talk*.

THE THREE'S DEADLY SIN

I wouldn't blame you if after reading these stories you pegged my dad as a poseur. But would you feel more compassion toward him if you knew he created and projected his shimmering image of success and achievement as defined by whatever crowd he was with because he believed that being, or at least looking, successful was the only way he could prove his worth and win love? Would your heart warm toward him if you knew that from the time he was a boy he thought he had to constantly craft his image to win other people's approval until eventually he couldn't tell the difference between his fake image and his authentic self anymore?

This is the Performer's snare.

According to the Enneagram, the deadly sin of the Performer is *deceit*—not because they deceive others as much as because they deceive themselves. As Nathaniel Hawthorne wrote, "No man, for any considerable period, can wear one face to himself and another to the multitude, without finally getting bewildered as to which may be the true."

In crafting a persona that will impress and perhaps even help them form relationships with high-influence people who can help them get ahead socially or professionally, Threes lose touch with who they authentically are. In time they so overidentify with their glittering persona that their true self gets lost in the performance. They, along with everyone else, are fooled into believing their false image is *who they really are.*

The strategy of projecting a false image to meet an unmet need is not unique to Threes. All of the numbers in the Feeling or Heart Triad (2, 3, 4) reject the idea that they can be seen for who they are and unconditionally loved, so they abandon their true selves to inhabit roles. Twos throw up a chirpy, likable image they can change in a heartbeat to please who they're with; Fours (spoiler alert!) project an image of uniqueness for reasons you'll learn about shortly; and Threes cast an image of success and achievement to win admiration.

FAMOUS THREES

Taylor Swift
Mitt Romney
Tom Cruise

Immature Threes need to win and make it look easy. For them, taking second place is a patronizing euphemism for being the first loser.

Whether they're in the classroom, on the athletic field, on a trading floor, on a stage, pastoring a megachurch, in the boardroom or serving the poor, Threes *have* to be the star. Because Threes grow up believing the world only values people for what they do rather than for who they are, becoming king or queen of the hill is a matter of life or death. Confusing success for love, Threes who lack self-awareness have to ace every test, close every deal, deliver a sermon that rivals the "I Have a Dream" speech every Sunday and break every corporate sales record. Life is all about racking up accomplishments that garner applause.

Threes are shape shifters who can switch personas to match the environment. "Threes don't have one persona, we are Legion," a pastor and now spiritually self-aware Three once half-joked with me. At a recent workshop a sharply dressed woman came up during a break after a talk on Threes and confessed, "My business partner swears she can hear the sound of my 'audience analysis software' launching in my brain when we walk into a room full of potential clients. Before the introductions are over I know exactly who I have to become to close the deal."

Unaware Threes are social chameleons. As you can imagine, however, their ability to create and project the image to make the sale or get the girl or guy can leave them wondering who their authentic self is. Once in a blue moon, when Threes slow down long enough to reflect on their lives, they might feel like they're a fraud. *I wear a thousand masks, but which is the authentic me?* When this flash of insight comes to them it surfaces a Three's worst fear: *What if there's no one behind the image? What if I'm no more than an empty suit?*

> "I like changing personalities."
>
> **MICK JAGGER**

Unless Threes have a wise spiritual adviser who helps them stay with that feeling of emptiness long enough to give their authentic self a chance to emerge, they will panic and retreat behind their persona again, this time redoubling their efforts to succeed and impress in order to mask their emptiness. More often than not it takes a fall on the scale of a Greek tragedy before a Three wakes up and realizes that "To thine own self be true" is a better life motto than "Image is everything."

ALL ABOUT THREES OR PERFORMERS

There's a lot to love about healthy Threes. They are optimistic, resilient people with audacious dreams who inspire others. When they're spiritually healthy and self-aware they have nothing to prove. They want to talk about your dreams and celebrate your accomplishments rather than flaunt their own achievements or sell you a line. There's not a hint of falseness about an evolved Three. They're no longer terrified of failure, and they share openly about what they've learned from their mistakes. They're generous and wise, and often volunteer their considerable skills to helping organizations be more effective at achieving their mission.

Yet there is a sad restlessness for unhealthy Threes—always striving, always keeping an eye out for advancement. Politically savvy and dressed to kill, they're

> "Image is everything."
>
> ***ANDRE AGASSI***

somehow always working a crowd as if asking, "How'm I doin'?" Some Threes get squirrelly when they have too much downtime in one place, so they need activity-based vacations like a scuba-diving trip or a bike trip across France, and good luck convincing them not to bring a briefcase full of work along with them. As Hurley and Donson note, sometimes Threes will pretend to be interested in conversations with people when they're not. If they know you're not "a player" or think you're not interesting enough, they will smile and nod like they're hanging on your every word when they're actually making a real estate deal or producing a record in their head or periodically glancing over your shoulder to see who and where the real players in the room are.

Recently Suzanne and I spoke at a conference where the audience was full of very successful men and women. One night a corporate lawyer in his mid-sixties named David shared with the group how he had once believed life was all about what you owned, who you knew and how good you looked, until at age fifty he had a "meet Jesus" crisis that brought him face-to-face with himself. "I've put a lot of effort into knowing and becoming my true self," David said, touching his hand to his heart. "Today I think far less about working and winning and more about 'David-ing.'"

David is a highly evolved Three. He no longer believes he has to work eighty-hour weeks and be widely acknowledged as the best at everything he does to be loved. In general, Threes have more difficulty recognizing and connecting to their feelings than any other number on the Enneagram. Not only do they not pick up on their own feelings, they won't pick up on yours very well either. Remember how we saw in the last chapter that Twos may be clueless about their own emotions but can zero in to yours with the accuracy of Doppler radar? Threes are just plain in the dark about feelings—their own and yours as well.

Threes *do* feelings more than *have* feelings. Because they can't access or recognize their feelings very well, Threes will unconsciously observe how other people are expressing their emotions and copy them. What gives away the fact that they aren't actually connecting to the sorrow they're visibly expressing at a funeral by looking sad is that they can be thinking about an unfinished work project at the same time.

Threes can mask and postpone feelings so they won't blow their "I have it all together" cover. In the moment, they can be feeling depressed, angry or scared and maintain their upbeat, confident poker face. At the end of the day, Threes care most about efficiency and completing a task. Feelings are messy, and they slow your progress toward your goal, so Threes don't spend too much time on them.

According to Riso and Hudson, the message Threes picked up in childhood is that it's not okay to have your own identity or feelings. As kids, Threes felt they needed to set aside their true selves to become the perfect prototype of whatever sort of person the important people in their lives associated with success. I once said to a Three in his spiritual journey, "How much you must have loved your father that you left your true self behind to please him." The man wept, as if relieved to know that love, not emptiness, lay behind his mask.

Here's a question: What would incentivize Threes to change in a culture that applauds and rewards them for embodying our cultural definition of success? *America is a Three country!* Countless numbers of us look at Threes and think, *Man, I wish I were him or her.* I say this because we are all complicit in perpetuating a world that encourages these wonderful folks to continue living in service to a lie. It's wrong of us to ask Threes to use their gifts to help grow our companies or raise money for our church's capital campaign—especially since when we're done using them, we turn around and criticize them behind their backs for being inauthentic or narcissistic. This is one reason Suzanne and I love the Enneagram. Doesn't knowing the worldview and motivation that drives a Three's personality help awaken in our hearts some compassion for their, and hopefully every other, number's plight?

We're awestruck when we meet a Three who is evolving spiritually despite having to get up every day and swim against the riptide of our success-oriented, image-obsessed culture. And there are plenty of these good people around doing the work of becoming themselves. They're saints in the making.

THREES AS CHILDREN

Early in life Threes pick up the wounding message "You are what you do." As a result they become high-performance achievement machines, striving to excel and be acknowledged for their accomplishments because they constitute the basis of their identity. If they sense their parents or culture prize academic achievement above all else, they'll set their sights on going to Harvard while they're still in middle school. Likewise, if Threes grow up in a culture or family where climbing the ranks of the Mafia to become a don represents ultimate success, then that will become their life's goal. Strange, I know, but it's contextual.

> "Our deepest calling is to grow into our own authentic selfhood, whether or not it conforms to some image of who we *ought* to be."
>
> **PARKER PALMER**

The saddest thing of all is how a Three will conform to their family's or culture's preferred image even if it means having to become someone who bears no resemblance to who they truly are or doing things that go against their nature. Tennis player Andre Agassi has a story like this. In 1991, Agassi appeared in a television ad for a camera called the Canon Rebel. In the commercial the cocky, fashionably attired super-athlete steps out of a white Lamborghini, casts an insouciant gaze toward the camera, lowers his Ray-Bans halfway down his nose and declares, "Image is everything." Oh, to be young and Three!

In his memoir, *Open,* Agassi describes growing up with a father whose love for him was tied to his performance on the court. Agassi shocked the world when in his book he publicly confessed for the first time that he had hated playing tennis from the time he first picked up a racket to the day he retired. What drove him to become a champion wasn't a passion for the game but his desire to win the heart of a father whom he describes as unable to "tell the difference between loving me and loving tennis." Other Threes describe growing up in homes where they worried that parents, peers or coaches would overlook or forget them if they didn't bring home extraordinary grades or trophies.

My friend Allen's parents grew up dirt poor. Growing up they repeatedly told Allen and his twin brother, "We want you to do more with your lives than we did with ours." Early on, when both kids began bringing home straight A's and excelling at basketball, Allen's mom and dad became so ecstatic and heaped so much praise on them that they felt they had no choice but to keep it up.

"My parents are great, and they loved us more than anything in the world," Allen says now. "They just had no idea how much pressure they were putting on us to succeed. It would break their hearts if they knew we grew up unconsciously believing their love for us was conditioned on our kicking ass at everything we did and how scared we were of disappointing them. They never once said, 'We'll only love you if you succeed!' But we were kids, and that's what we unconsciously heard." Sadly, the unlived lives of parents sometimes push their children toward destinies not of their own choosing.

Kids who are Threes wake up in the morning with a plan for their day. Socially aware, they know what they're going to wear to school and who they'll sit with at lunch. They know who the cool kids are and may go against their own feelings or wishes in order to be accepted in their circle. These kids come tricked out with all the onboard equipment they need to achieve and succeed.

They try to do the things that are valued by the people around them, and they take it hard when they fail. They are focused and naturally competitive because they believe they are loved for their achievements. These are the kids who want to stand out. And they do.

THREES IN RELATIONSHIPS

As the number least in touch with their feelings on the Enneagram, it only makes sense that Threes would have things to work out in the relationship department.

As part of their larger self-marketing campaign, spiritually unaware Threes will want to project the image of the perfect family to the outside world, but keeping up appearances can exhaust their partners and kids. Out of touch with their feelings and eager to make the right impression, Threes can consciously or unconsciously act the role of the quintessential devoted parent and spouse. Other Threes on autopilot can unconsciously view their partner or their relationship with them like an action item on their task-management list. Those people can become one of the many projects they're working on at any given time. For instance, you might hear Threes talk about how they and their partner sit down once a year to set spiritual, financial, physical or social goals for their marriage or relationship or to discuss ways in which they can make the day-to-day management of the family more efficient or productive. Clearly being intentional about relationships is admirable, so long as they remain spiritual unions we cultivate, not business partnerships we manage.

Without exception, the relationships of spiritually unevolved Threes suffer because they're almost all workaholics. They have so many projects running and so many goals to achieve they can't give their undivided attention to people they love. As Helen Palmer remarks, a "Three's heart is in their work," so whatever feelings they have are used toward accomplishing a goal or task, and there's not much left over for other people.

Threes have a supernatural talent for multitasking. They can simultaneously juggle driving, closing a multimillion-dollar deal on their cell phone, eating a sandwich, listening to an audiobook version of David Allen's bestseller *Getting Things Done*, and conversing with their spouse about a problem one of the kids is having at school. It's not merely impressive, it's Cirque du Soleil impressive, unless you're their partner, child or friend who feels devalued and less important than the Three's ambitions.

Because Threes alter their appearance to win over different types of people, they keep their circles of friends separate from one another. If they threw a party and mistakenly invited all their friends from the different spheres of their lives they'd lose their minds—no one can change hats that fast.

Threes prize friendships that are free and undemanding. Life is all about getting things done, so Threes steer away from high-maintenance, complicated or demanding friendships that take time and energy away from accomplishing goals.

The defensive strategy of Threes is identification. Threes defend themselves against harm by completely immersing themselves in the task they're performing, or equating their identity with their title and the institutions for which they work. Because of this, Threes will defend their firm's reputation or the crazy number of hours they spend at the office to the death.

As Richard Rohr observes, the saddest number on the Enneagram is an unsuccessful Three, one whose ambitions were greater than their talent. I would add that it's heartbreaking to meet Threes in the second half of life who never woke up to their own game. It's a terrible thing to be seated next to a seventy-year-old guy at a dinner party who is still dropping names, telling you where he went to college or boasting about how young he was when he made partner and how much money he cashed out with at retirement.

THREES AT WORK

If it's not clear already, Threes feel most in their element at work. More than any other type, they crave achievement and recognition, and for most adults that means killing it at their job. For Threes who don't work outside the home, like stay-at-home parents, their natural tendency to hunt for external validation can emerge in other ways, such as comparing notes about whose kids figured out potty training in utero and were accepted early decision to Princeton while they were still in pre-K.

Choosing success over substance, Threes are revered in America. They're avatars of an American ideal—the smart, charismatic, ambitious, type-A man or woman. But be careful.

> "Work is more fun than fun!"
> **NOEL COWARD**

There's a fine line between a type and a stereotype. Some folks think all Threes are like the character Don Draper from the AMC series *Mad Men*. Could a Three who isn't spiritually mature become a success-crazed, image-obsessed high achiever who charms and claws his or her way up to the top of the corporate food chain, or a smile-flashing, glad-handing candidate stumping for votes at a state fair? Sure, but those are more stereotypes—widely held, formulaic caricatures of a particular kind of person. Threes are people, not clichés. Like all of us, they're complicated, and they come in an infinite variety of shades and tones. They're not all CEOS or celebrities, nor do they aspire to be. They show up in almost every profession, from music to the mission field. They can be anyone from David Bowie to Dorothy Day, the founder of the Catholic Worker Movement. But they all believe the same lie: you're only as *loved* as your last success.

As a university professor friend of mine once told me, "Come listen in to the conversations that take place between professors at a faculty meeting at my school. When they're not reminding each other where they earned their PhDs, they're dropping the name of the prestigious journal that recently published one of their articles, mentioning the invitation they've just received to give the plenary address at a well-known academic conference or jockeying for tenure."

When they're spiritually healthy, these charismatic, productive, go-get-'em folks are authentic, visionary leaders and extraordinary builders who deserve our admiration. Like every number, though, when they're not mature and don't know their blind spots they're an accident looking for an intersection.

People will say Threes are willing to do whatever it takes to get ahead. They care about titles, who's next in line for promotion and who occupies the corner office. Threes make phenomenal salespeople, though they develop a kind of pride around their ability to turn it on and become whomever the customer wants them to be to make the sale.

Because status matters so much to Threes, so do status symbols. When they build equity they find out which toys message success in their setting and go get them. If they're investment bankers or professional athletes, it might be boats, second homes or Teslas. If they're social justice advocates they'll wear extra tattered clothing as part of a campaign to showcase their commitment to living in solidarity with the poor.

Threes' issues with feelings become really clear when you see them at work. They live for setting a goal, killing it, setting another goal, killing it, setting the next goal, killing it. This is where Threes get their energy, but it costs them. Imagine a Three is working on an important project at work when their spouse or a friend calls to say they're feeling angry or upset with them about something. The Three might have feelings about the situation as well, but having to deal with feelings threatens their ability to complete their project on schedule. So they disconnect in order to stay focused on work. It's as if they say, *I'm going to slip this emotion into my "Feelings to Deal with Later" file and come back to it when I'm finished with this task.*

How often do you think Threes go back to deal with the feeling? Rarely. Once that project is done they're on to the next one. By midlife, what do you think a Three's "Feelings to Deal with Later" file looks like? If it hasn't already burst, it's definitely overflowing. A Three's ability to postpone or set feelings aside explains why people often experience them as superficial, emotionally shallow and difficult to connect with. Productivity, efficiency, goals and measurable results—these are what Threes care about and do better than anyone else, particularly efficiency. Threes want to get to the finish line of a project or task as quickly as possible, and this desire for efficiency affects relationships and decisions.

Threes are pragmatic. They'll do whatever it takes to get the job done. To achieve a goal a Three might cut corners for the sake of expediency, which can hurt the quality of their work. They're not necessarily unethical, but they might embellish or leave out a few facts to secure a position, angle for a promotion or close a deal. As a songwriter I occasionally did work with a successful publisher in New York City who was a textbook Three. One day I asked a fellow songwriter whether he thought this likeable but shrewd publisher was a straight-up guy. He laughed and said, "Doug's not a liar but he'll 'sculpt' the truth if he has to."

Threes often run people over on the way to the goal line, which they may or may not apologize for. They demand loyalty from their employees, so if your boss happens to be an immature Three, I wouldn't openly question her decision to introduce a new product line unless you want to watch its big launch from the penalty box.

Enthusiastic and confident, a Three's talk style is *promotion* or sales. Threes would rather say too little than too much. They love selling people on an idea, the company they work for, the product they sell, the cause they champion, the hobby they enjoy.

Threes are charismatic, and because they're adaptive and attuned to what others want from them, they know exactly what to say to inspire and motivate the people who work for them. They gravitate toward careers where moving up is dependent on making good impressions and where promotions are handed out to those who best embody the values of the company or people they work for.

WINGS

Threes with a Four wing (3w4). It's difficult to be a Three with a Four wing. Fours, as we'll see in the next chapter, are Romantics who care greatly about depth and authenticity. These people take having a rich inner life to a whole new level. Because Threes can be chameleons and Fours value authenticity, 3w4s experience tremendous confusion and interior dissonance. At the same time they're projecting an image to please the crowd, the Four wing is pointing at them and screaming, "Phony! Fraud!" Threes with Four wings are more introspective and in touch with their shame and other feelings than 3w2s. They're sensitive, artistic, emotionally intense, and they work more carefully on "crafting" the right image. Threes with Four wings aren't as driven to be stars as 3w2s, but they can be more pretentious.

Threes with a Two wing (3w2). Charming and intimate, 3w2s make great entertainers, politicians, salespeople and pastors. When their lust for attention and recognition overtakes them or when they feel unappreciated, however, they can become angry and hostile. More than 3w4s, they need to be stars.

They actually embody some of the characteristics they have employed in an effort to be seen as more loving, generous and kind. These Threes still have a strong desire to be recognized for their achievements, but they also use some of their energy to help other people be successful.

STRESS AND SECURITY

Stress. When Threes get stressed they take on characteristic behaviors of unhealthy Nines. They retreat to the couch with the remote or lose themselves in unproductive busywork. Seemingly worn out, they lose their characteristic optimism and confidence and become self-doubtful. Lacking motivation, stressed-out Threes might lose interest in working out, eating healthy food and paying attention to their appearance.

Security. When Threes are feeling secure they move to the positive side of Six, where they become warmer and more in touch with their feelings and the feelings of others. Less competitive and defensive, Threes in this space have more energy to devote to family and friends. No longer needing to be the star or in control, they care more about what's best for the group and want to connect to something that's bigger than they are. Threes who are connected to the positive side of Six can finally experience being loved for who they are instead of for what they do.

SPIRITUAL TRANSFORMATION

Being a Three and living in America is like being an alcoholic living above a saloon. In our success- and image-obsessed culture they are more revered and rewarded than any other number on the Enneagram. Is it any wonder spiritual work is hard for them? Because the adaptive strategies of their personality work so well and for so long, they might not start working on themselves spiritually until midlife, or when they fail and can't cover it up.

Inevitably as Threes awaken spiritually and become self-aware, they will feel naked and ashamed. There's no getting around it. In that moment, what they need is a kind but strong friend who will call them back to the truth of who they are, should they start marketing and packaging themselves for mass consumption again. Actually, we all need at least one friend who can encourage us in the struggle to become ourselves. It's not work one should do alone.

We all need to hear we are loved for who we are, but Threes need to hear it until the day comes when they look in the mirror and see not an image so much as the reflection of a son or daughter of God. The healing message for Threes is "You are loved just for who you are." Angels sing when this message penetrates a Three's heart.

TEN PATHS TO TRANSFORMATION FOR THREES

1. It's important for every number to develop a practice of silence, solitude and meditation, but it's particularly essential for Threes since you place such high value on activity and productivity.

2. Find a spiritual director to accompany you on your journey to reclaim your authentic self. It's hard to walk the path alone.

3. Challenge your definition of success, and craft a new one based on your feelings, desires and values, not those inherited from family or culture.

4. Don't wait until you have an affair, become an alcoholic or are the youngest person in your family to have a heart attack before you ask the question, "Who am I if I'm not my persona?" Do it now.

5. Material success and being real are not mutually exclusive. Success is great if the person responsible for it is the real you.

6. Take an inventory of who and what gets sacrificed while you're frantically racing to cross the finish line first—spouse, kids, health, friendships.

7. Take a vacation and *do not bring work with you.*

8. Try being just another bozo on the bus. Resist the temptation to take the leadership rein or to be the center of attention. Instead, try being a collaborative team member who wants to help others shine and succeed.

9. Have at least one close friend with whom you can be real and vulnerable. As a Three, you probably have a lot of friends, but make sure some of them are people who can love you when you're a complete disaster, not just when you're projecting an image of success.

10. Read Richard Rohr's books *Falling Upward: A Spirituality for the Two Halves of Life* and *Immortal Diamond: The Search for Our True Self.*

WHAT IT'S LIKE TO BE A FOUR

1. I like things that are unconventional, dramatic and refined. I'm definitely not a fan of the ordinary.

2. I never really felt like I belonged.

3. I have so many feelings in a day it's hard to know which ones to pay attention to first.

4. Some people think I am aloof, but I'm really just unique.

5. In social situations I tend to hang back and wait for others to approach me.

6. Melancholy is comfortable for me, so it's annoying when people try to cheer me up.

7. I'm not like everyone else . . . phew.

8. I'm very sensitive to criticism, and it takes me a while to get over it.

9. I spend a lot of time trying to explain myself.

10. When people tell me what to do I'm often tempted to do the opposite.

11. Sometimes I just disappear and go radio silent for a few days.

12. I'm okay with sad songs, sad stories and sad movies. Overly happy people give me a headache.

13. I feel there is something essential lacking in me.

14. It's really hard for me to settle into a relationship because I'm always looking for my ideal soul mate.

15. I'm self-conscious. It's hard for me to find my place in a room full of people.

16. People say I'm too intense and my feelings overwhelm them.

17. I'm either an artist or highly creative. I come up with one amazing, creative idea after another. It's executing them that's hard.

18. Lots of people misunderstand me, and it makes me frustrated.

19. I pull people in, but then I get nervous and push them away.

20. I worry a lot about abandonment.

8

TYPE FOUR

THE ROMANTIC

*If you've ever had that feeling of loneliness,
of being an outsider, it never quite leaves you.*

TIM BURTON

Healthy Fours have a considerable emotional range, and they manage it by not speaking or acting on every feeling they have. They know they don't have to be special to win God's unconditional love. These Fours have found a way to live, for the most part, outside the pattern of shame and inferiority. They are deeply creative, emotionally honest and connected, and attuned to beauty.

Average Fours struggle daily with learning to accept themselves as they are. Such efforts are complicated as they seek their identity by exaggerating their uniqueness. These Fours are coy; they want you to want them but they play hard to get. Their melancholy often goes unchecked, causing painful distance between themselves and others. Average Fours are moody, melodramatic, needy and self-pitying.

Unhealthy Fours tend to be manipulative, playing the role of victim in order to create or maintain relationships. They find themselves lacking when compared to others, which only exacerbates their self-debasement. These Fours feel so much shame they are unable to connect to the very part of themselves that believes they can change and be better.

Shortly before our first child, Cailey, was born, Anne began to research baby strollers. Like us, most of our friends were in their late twenties and either pregnant or popping babies out like vending machines. There was no shortage of people to ask for advice.

"Everyone says we should buy a Graco," Anne announced over dinner one night.

"Everyone?" I replied, arching one eyebrow.

I don't like it when someone says I should do something on the basis that everyone else is. During their yearly migration, thousands of Norwegian lemmings commit mass suicide because everyone they know is doing it.

"Couldn't we be more creative?" I asked.

"It's a stroller, not a prom dress," Anne said, using her "I'm eight months pregnant so don't screw with me" voice.

"Noted," I said, quickly dropping the subject.

However, the next morning while flipping through baby catalogs I happened upon an ad for a cool stroller. Sure, it was expensive, and the manufacturer would have to ship it to us from their factory in England, but it was for our first child, right? I ordered one immediately.

"Are you crazy?" Anne objected when I told her the news. "We could drive to Sears right now and buy a Graco for half the price."

"We're having a *girl*. Don't you want her to have an English pram?"

"A *pram*?" Anne scoffed, shaking her head in disbelief as she turned on her heels and walked out of the room. "Mr. 'I Gotta Be Me' strikes again."

"Wait until you see it," I promised. "You'll thank me."

Three days before Anne's due date the box containing our new pram appeared on our doorstep. I was eager to unveil and admire it until I saw the words "Assembly Required" writ large across the side of the carton

When it comes to being handy I'm genetically challenged. In fact, a career counselor once informed me that my spatial visualization and finger dexterity scores were more like those of a clam than a human being. "Feel free to write songs about tools, just don't pick one up," he advised. "You'll hurt someone."

I put aside my counselor's warning and took a deep breath. "I can do this," I declared over and over while dragging the box into the house.

Once inside I laid out the pieces to the pram on my living room floor. Holding the instruction manual open in one hand and scratching my head with the other, I surveyed the sea of nuts and bolts, springs, plastic fasteners, and other curious miscellanea at my feet. There were so many parts I wondered whether I was expected to assemble a pram or a Boeing 747.

Not one to back away from a challenge, I vowed I would have the pram ready to roll by the time Anne arrived home from work. But a few hours later she found me slumped on the couch, staring at the ceiling and strumming a plaintive lament on my guitar like Leonard Cohen having a bad day.

"This is a metaphor for my life," I moaned, gesturing toward the unfinished stroller lying on its side on our living room floor, its bare axle sticking up in the air, as if flipping me the bird. "I'm hopeless."

Anne smiled and sat next to me on the couch. "You're a torture to yourself," she said, patting my hand.

It wasn't the last time Anne has told me that over the course of our marriage. After all, I'm a Four on the Enneagram.

THE FOUR'S DEADLY SIN

Fours feel something important is missing from their essential makeup.

They're not sure what it is, whether it was taken from them or they had it long ago but lost it—only that the missing part is nowhere to be found and they're to blame. The result is that they feel "different," ashamed, uncertain about who they are and ill at ease in the world.

When I was twelve a bicycle repairman told me that my wobbly front tire was "out of true," an expression I had never heard before but immediately recognized as describing not just the bike but myself. Out of true. That's how a Four feels.

Fours believe they alone have this tragic flaw, so when they compare themselves to others (which is all the time), they feel inferior. As Richard Rohr puts it, Fours often feel "ruled by a hidden shame." The joy and completeness others seem to enjoy is a daily reminder of what they themselves lack.

There's a scene in the film version of *Wuthering Heights* that marvelously portrays a Four's inner sense of abandonment, loss and separation. The main characters, Catherine and Heathcliff, are standing outside the home of their wealthy neighbors, the Lintons, who are hosting a party. With their noses pressed up against the window glass, Catherine and Heathcliff watch the elegantly dressed guests dance and laugh the night away. It's clear from the plaintive expressions on their faces that they wish they could join the festivities, but this is as close as they're going to get. They're outsiders.

FAMOUS FOURS

Amy Winehouse
Thomas Merton
Vincent van Gogh

Like Heathcliff and Catherine, Fours yearn to join the party of life, but the absence of that fundamental *something* disqualifies them from getting an invitation. They've been exiled to the Island of Misfit Toys through some nameless fault of their own.

It's no surprise that *envy* is the deadly sin of Fours. They envy the normalcy, happiness and sense of comfort with which others seem to move through life. They instantly spot who has a more interesting life, a happier family or childhood story, a better job, superior taste, a more privileged education, more distinguishing clothes or unrivaled artistic talent. This envy, coupled with their pervasive sense of "irredeemable deficiency," launches Fours on a never-ending quest to find the missing piece without which they never feel at home in the world. Sadly, by fixating on what's missing, Fours are blind to what's present in their lives, namely the many wonderful qualities they already possess.

In case you were wondering, envy and jealousy are different. Envy has to do with desiring a characteristic others possess, while jealousy occurs when we feel like something we already possess is at risk of being taken away from us. Though envy is their big sin, Fours experience jealousy as well. For them, jealousy has to do with their fear of abandonment and expresses itself in the possessiveness they feel toward the people they love.

ALL ABOUT FOURS OR ROMANTICS

As you might guess, Fours are prone to melancholy. Like the Old Testament figure Job they can steep in lament. After all, it's hard to be chipper when the now-dated U2 song "Still Haven't Found What I'm Looking For" or the Radiohead song "Creep" play like the soundtrack in the movie of your life.

Don't, however, mistake melancholy for depression. The Four's pining and wistfulness has a bittersweet quality to it. If back in my twenties you gave me the choice between going on an all-expenses-paid trip to Disney World or to the west of Ireland where I could sit atop a cliff overlooking the sea and write songs, I'd have taken Ireland in a heartbeat. As Victor Hugo, the author of *Les Misérables*, once wrote, "Melancholy is the happiness of being sad."

Unfortunately, the Four's melancholy can spiral into melodrama. A Four can take a minor tiff with a friend and turn it into a Wagner opera, while a breakup with a girlfriend or boyfriend can rival a scene from *Dr. Zhivago*. All these theatrics often push away the people with whom the Four most wants to make a heartfelt connection. As is the case with every type on the Enneagram, the strategies we employ to get our needs met so often work against us.

You would think, given their desire to fit in and belong, that Fours would want to try to be like everyone else to blend in more, but that's the last thing Fours want. The need of the Four is *to be special or unique*. They believe the only way they can recapture or compensate for their missing piece and finally secure an authentic identity is by cultivating a unique image, one that distinguishes them from everyone else. Perhaps then people will love and accept them and they can return from their exile on the Island of Misfit Toys.

The Four's need to be special was never clearer to me than during a premarital counseling session I had with a couple named Roger and Linda. Roger, a skilled chiropractor, wasn't surprised when he learned he was a One. Linda thought she might be a Four but wasn't sure, so I described to her what Fours were like. Halfway through, the lights went on.

"Wait, there are other people just like me?" she wailed, like I'd told her she had six weeks to live.

"Well, sort of, but—"

"That can't be. I thought I was *different*," she said, burying her face in her hands and sobbing uncontrollably.

Most Fours could teach Anguish as a Second Language. They're drawn to all things tragic, and their talk style is *lament*. They can play the role of the tragic romantic, or sometimes the artist who suffers for their art, and they can always be counted on to tell sad stories. I don't talk about suffering or sad topics all the time, but when I do it doesn't seem to have the same depressive effect on me that it does on others. In fact, sad stories move me as long as they're honest and not sentimental. The dark, intense emotions they arouse help me explore my own depths and find meaning. Over the years, however, I've learned not everyone sees the world through the same lens I do. Back in 1990 I thought director Tim Burton's then-new film *Edward Scissorhands* sounded like the perfect movie to take a girl out to see on a first date. Turns out it wasn't for everybody.

Fours are the most complex of all the types on the Enneagram; what you see is never what you get. There are always more layers of things going on underneath the surface. Their waters run deep. *Who am I? What's my purpose? How does the narrative of my life fit into the grand scheme of things?* These are the angsty, existential, reading-Albert-Camus-on-a-rainy-day kinds of questions that occupy a Four.

As you can imagine, Fours wrestle with dissatisfaction. They always want the unavailable. What they have is never what they really want, and what they want is always somewhere "out there" just beyond their reach. If only they knew that what they want is inside them.

Fours don't have feelings; they *are* their feelings. Their feelings form the basis of their identity. Who on earth would they be without them? However, Fours aren't satisfied with having regular, run-of-the-mill feelings; they want *supersized* feelings.

As a younger man, I never met an emotion I didn't want to embellish or intensify. If I felt good, I wanted to feel ecstatic, so I'd play a Sinatra big band record and invite ten friends to dinner at the last minute. If I felt blue and introspective, I would listen to Samuel Barbers "Adagio for Strings"—anything to adrenalize whatever I was feeling in the moment.

Given their love and overidentification with charged emotions, the Four's mood is in a constant state of flux. They swing from one feeling state to another as deftly and quickly as a monkey swings from one tree branch to the next. As author Tom Condon points out, a Four's issues and emotional landscape aren't much different from those of a teenager. Both share "the sense of alienation, their conscious search for identity, their preoccupation with who they are as unique from others, a tendency to romanticize death, the conviction that no else has ever felt what they feel, and a keen awareness of both the elation and pain of love."

So. Spot. On.

Fours' moods are like fast-moving weather patterns. In the blink of an eye they can go from up to down, back to average, then plummet, then soar and finally return to baseline. In fact, Fours can feel overwhelmed from experiencing so many feelings at one time that when it comes time to organize them, they don't know which one to pick out and talk about first. Do you see the problem? If the identity of the Four is hitched to their feelings, then it's always changing. Their sense of self never stabilizes. Until they wake up it's like watching someone riding the emotional equivalent of the El Diablo roller coaster at Six Flags.

Fours have rich imaginations and fantasy lives, where they go to reflect and pine about the past. Fours spend lots of time longingly looking back on their childhoods saying, "If only, if only," or "What if?" When they're not fantasizing about the past, they're imagining a future when they'll live in the perfect place, have the ideal job, have the right set of friends or finally be completed by their soul mate.

> "I am solitary as grass. What is it I miss? Shall I ever find it, whatever it is?"
>
> **SYLVIA PLATH**

Life is a Catch-22 for Fours. They want to belong in the world, but they feel deficient. So they compensate for what they sense they lack by projecting a special image, which leads to them acting out in ways that only makes fitting in harder. Take my friend Don, a remarkable songwriter and a poster-child Four. When he was in eighth grade Don and his family moved from Missouri to Kansas.

Though only four hours apart, it might as well have been a parallel universe across the globe. After trying and failing to make friends with the popular kids at his new school, Don changed course. It began with him riding to school on a yellow moped, wearing a red helmet with toy gun sucker darts stuck to the top like a pair of antenna, his black Samsonite briefcase affixed to the back with a bungee cord. Some days he'd show up for class wearing his father's Air Force flight suit and a pair of science goggles.

Do you see how all these eccentric, compensatory behaviors worked against Don's desired goal of achieving social acceptance? Though sucker darts and flight suits might not be your thing, Fours are known for wearing clothes that set them apart and attract attention. Fours will make it look like they just threw it together, but trust me: it was well thought out.

The search for authenticity means everything to Fours, and they can spot a poseur from a mile away. Reading J. D. Salinger's *Catcher in the Rye* in high school was a watershed moment for me because I so identified with the main character Holden Caulfield's contempt for "phonies." I can't tell you how many Fours tell me they had the exact same reaction. We don't like mediocrity, superficiality or people who are unsparingly optimistic all the time. My daughter reminds me that when she was sixteen she whined at the dinner table, "I just want to be happy," to which I replied, "Where did you acquire this taste for luxury?" I like happiness, but given the state of the world, who can expect perpetual glee? Besides, people who haven't suffered or are always happy are less interesting than shrubbery.

Fours are people who are attracted to the offbeat and avant-garde in life. They care deeply about beauty and art. They decorate their homes in a way that reflects their originality and create things that give expression to their feelings and slant vision of the world. They take up unusual hobbies and often have a wildly interesting and diverse group of friends.

All of these elite interests can give people the impression that Fours are snobbish or aloof. To be honest, we occasionally view ourselves as superior to the huddling masses who we think have shallow feelings or substandard taste, or that we're exempt from pedestrian chores like doing the laundry or raking leaves when we're preoccupied with larger questions of life, but sometimes our standing off to the side of the crowd is more an invitation to notice and come over to connect with us than anything else.

Fours find meaning best expressed through imagery, metaphors, story and symbols that can express feelings and truths that test the limits of language. As an Episcopal priest living in Nashville I see more than a few Fours on Sunday mornings. We love liturgical churches where incense, bells, statues, icons, sacraments, colored vestments and pageantry satisfy our appreciation for mystery and transcendence.

And don't get us started on martyrs. Fours love us some martyrs.

FOURS AS CHILDREN

Fours often say they felt different and misunderstood by their parents, siblings and peers growing up. My older brothers were rough-and-tumble guys who didn't shy away from the occasional playground brawl while I was physically small and more intro-spective. They played football and roughhoused, while I played guitar and read P. G. Wodehouse. They went to Catholic school, and I belonged at Hogwarts. I definitely grew up feeling like a bastard at a family reunion.

As children Fours seem to be both approachable and unavailable at the same time. They live with a sense that they are not like other children so they try to make a place for themselves by capitalizing on their differences. That often backfires, sabotaging their chances of getting what they really want, which is a sense of belonging.

The wounding message Fours hear all the time is "There's some-thing off about you. No one understands you, and you'll never belong." These kids feel lonely and misunderstood most of the time. They desperately want people to "get them," but the often eccentric ways they use to communicate who they are and how they see the world make them all the more incomprehensible to people. The present seems unbearable at times, and the future is fraught with anxiety, so they think a lot about the past. They try to figure where they lost that missing piece, how things might have been different and why God abandoned them. If you see a Four looking off with that longing, 100-mile stare and breathing glottal sighs, they're probably playing the "What if? . . . What if? . . . What if?" refrain in their head. Call it what you will, but those little brains and hearts grow up and become Fours like Bob Dylan, Meryl Streep, choreographer Martha Graham and Swedish film director Ingmar Bergman, so let's not rush to say to them, "Why can't you be like other kids?"

FOURS IN RELATIONSHIPS

Relationships are the stage on which the drama of a Four's life unfolds. They can be high-maintenance friends or partners. They are always scouting around for the ideal someone who will help them overcome their feeling of unworthiness and complete them. That's a lot to ask.

Fours are intense. They want to dig down to the heart to deal with whatever's going on between you and them. If they're on an emotional mountaintop, they want you to be there with them, and if they're feeling low and morbidly self-interested, they might invite you over so they can share their woes over a bottle of wine in the hope that you can fix them.

Fours can leverage trivial events or situations into opportunities to show off their Shakespearean flair. When their demand for peak emotional experiences exceeds supply, they might instigate a drama with friend or a partner, then after several weeks of silence extend an awkward apology in the form of a poem or song they've written and performed on your voicemail. Their penchant for theatrical behavior can earn them a reputation for being drama queens or crisis kings. For some people the Four's highs are a little too high, their lows a little too low. It can be tiring.

Fours are also a challenge in relationships because they're concerned about re-experiencing the abandonment they endured or perceive they endured as children. This anxiety plays itself out in what Helen Palmer describes as a push-pull dance. Looking back, there were times, particularly in our early marriage, when I would unconsciously start to think, *Maybe I love this woman too much. What if I lose her, or worse, what if she leaves me? I couldn't endure it.*

Once this fear of abandonment set in I would unconsciously begin to push Anne away, emotionally distancing myself from her by dwelling on her faults, being vaguely critical, ruminating on what was missing in our marriage or withholding affection. After a few hours or weeks I'd wake up and panic, thinking to myself, *Oh no, I've gone too far. I adore this woman, and the last thing I want to do is lose her.* So I'd run back to pull Anne in, saying things like, "I love you so much. I'm here for you. Are you here for me?"

> "What does all this mean finally, I kept asking like a college kid. Why does it make me want to cry? Maybe it's that we are all outsiders, we are all making our own unusual way through a wilderness of normality that is just a myth."
>
> **ANNE RICE**

Another variation on the push-pull dance happens when Fours say to themselves, *If I could only find the right partner, the right therapist, the right church or the right friend, then I'd be complete.* Once Fours find this perfect someone or something they'll pull them in until they get close enough to realize that whoever or whatever it is won't fill the hole in their soul. Then the Four will push them away. Maybe they stop returning calls or showing up for things without explanation. But then when the same person begins to move too far away from them, they start to desire them again.

More than anything else what Fours need are partners and friends who know how to "detach without withdrawing." You have to be able to listen without necessarily agreeing with them. If you love a Four, you can't allow yourself to get sucked into their swirling emotional vortex. You have to remain detached and let Fours do their thing until they're done—but whatever you do, unless they're really crazy, don't leave them. If you do, it only confirms their worst fear, which is that they are "irredeemably deficient." Fours in relationship need to have their feelings acknowledged and need their loved ones to understand that melancholy is not depression. People who love Fours can help them by encouraging them to look at both the positive and negative sides of things

As is true with all types, when Enneagram Fours are mature, healthy and self-aware they make wonderful friends, coworkers and partners. They're hard working, generous and marvelously creative. They'll awaken you to the beauty and transcendent nature of the world by guiding you into emotions you would otherwise never dare to feel. As artists, they can say clearly what you always felt vaguely. Meditate on van Gogh's *Starry Night over the Rhone* or listen to Sufjan Stevens's record *Carrie and Lowell* or Prince's *Purple Rain*, and you'll appreciate the Four's gift for guiding people into or through necessary emotional waters they would never otherwise dare wade into alone.

You know how when you're in pain you want someone to be with you who won't try to fix you or make you feel better? When you're in that spot, reach out to a Four. They're more empathic than any other type. Fours instinctively know how to honor and bear witness to the pain of others. They know there's nothing they can do to help other than be in solidarity with you until whatever afflictive emotion you're experiencing has finished its work in you. So when your dog needs to be put to sleep and you can't bear the idea of going to the vet alone, don't call a Two. They'll show up with a casserole and a new puppy. Fours will drive you to the vet's, stand alongside you and help hold the dog during those final moments, and give you nothing other than the ministry of their presence. There's no such thing as a Four who can't sit shiva. That said, Fours can be incredibly funny people. Their weird take on the world and sense of irony can produce outrageous, comedic moments.

FOURS AT WORK

As you might imagine, many Fours gravitate toward careers in the arts. A disproportionate percentage of our most beloved actors, poets, novelists, musicians, dancers, painters and filmmakers are Fours on the Enneagram. But Fours don't exclusively choose arts-related career paths. They can be anything from a chef to a yoga teacher to a worship pastor to a web designer. Because Fours are comfortable accompanying people on their journeys through painful times, they make great therapists, pastoral counselors and spiritual directors. They'll thrive as long as their work affords them the opportunity to express their creativity, depth of feeling and distinct style.

If you want Fours to perform ordinary or routine tasks, forget it. First, they'll feel it's beneath their sensibilities. Fours will procrastinate if you ask them to tackle projects that involve too many details, like writing reports or fussing around with spreadsheets. If you meet a Four whose day job is waiting tables or driving a cab, chances are it's a side gig to support their art or some other creative passion.

To feel fulfilled, a Four's work has to have a higher purpose, make use of and highlight their area of expertise, tap into their fertile imagination and interior life, and make it possible for them to establish emotional connections with others. They dislike uniformity, regulation, and an abundance of rules and expectations.

Fours aren't always great on teams where their gifts might get buried in the mix. They want to be seen and appreciated for bringing unique perspectives. They won't necessarily be resentful if you don't implement something they suggest as long as it's clear you heard and understood their idea. Sure, they're temperamental, but if you give them something special to do and let them go, they'll often outperform your expectations.

As Helen Palmer cautions, when it comes time for a Four's performance review, avoid saying things to them like, "Why can't you write copy like Andrew does?" If you do, the Four will spend the rest of the day feeling envious of Andrew instead of focusing on the copy you want them to write.

As leaders Fours make decisions on the basis of feelings and intuition, which can freak data-oriented people out, and they lead by force of personality, which can intimidate the people who work for them. Their ability to bring compatible people together and create a climate of collaboration versus competition is invaluable. They're inspiring and bring out what's special in others.

Unfortunately, the push-pull dance of the Four occurs not only in personal relationships but in the workplace as well. One day they'll treat you like Employee of the Month and the next day they may squint at you and act as if you're a recent hire. Don't worry, they'll be back—it's just part of the dance.

Finally, if you work for a Four, be real. Inauthentic or frivolous people are invisible to them.

WINGS

Fours with a Three wing (4w3). Fours are sandwiched between the Performer (Three) on the one hand and the Observer (Five) on the other. Fours with a dominant Three wing want to be both the most unique *and* the best. Their energy is competitive, and they have enough of the Three's image-consciousness that they are more aware than other Fours of the need to dial back their emotional intensity and quirky idiosyncrasies to be socially acceptable. With the added energy of the Three, two things are likely: first, they will be more outgoing, which translates to overly dramatic; and second, they are usually more productive, turning dreams and ideas into reality. Both of these tendencies show the Four's desire to be noticed. Often these Fours have more frequent mood swings than Fours with a Five wing.

Fours with a Five wing (4w5). Fours with a Five wing are likely more introverted and unconventional. They are very concerned with uniqueness, but they have less need to be noticed by an audience than 4w3. They are quietly different, often eccentric. They spend more time alone and find it easier to let their emotions be without having to talk about them or respond with some kind of action.

STRESS AND SECURITY

Stress. Fours in stress will begin to look and act like unhealthy Twos. Here they repress their own needs and become excessively dependent on others. Craving attention, they'll need a ton of reassurance and affirmation from friends and partners, and jealousy might surface.

Security. Fours in security take on the traits of a healthy One, where they stop talking about their creative ideas and actually become disciplined enough to buckle down and realize them. They are more aware of what's happening in the present, more centered and calm. When Fours are connected to the positive side of One they are much more successful in relationships, knowing they can have feelings without talking about them or acting on them. This is a very mature place for Fours.

SPIRITUAL TRANSFORMATION

All their lives, Fours have felt different and separate from others. Is it any wonder they came to believe they could only recapture the love they yearn for by becoming unique and special? Their sense of identity has never been quite stable, as they've tried on one after another like suits looking for the right fit. Fours shouldn't be angry with themselves, since everyone has peculiar, counterintuitive strategies for getting their needs met.

So first, Fours need to hear this loud and clear: there's nothing missing. It may be hard to believe, but God didn't ship them here with a vital part absent from their essential makeup. Fours arrived on life's doorstep with the same equipment everyone else did. The kingdom is inside them too. Everything they need is here.

As part of the Feeling Triad, the Four's journey toward spiritual health and vitality will involve doing some work in this realm. They must learn how to regulate and stabilize their emotions. It's hard at first, but Fours must figure out how to observe and detach from their feelings rather than exaggerate them, wallow in them or act them out impulsively. To do this Fours need to cultivate what's called *equanimity*, a sorely ignored virtue in the Christian tradition. Equanimity refers to the ability to remain emotionally composed and steady regardless of what's happening around us. Remember, feelings are like waves on the surface of the ocean. Don't attach or identify with them but with the vast ocean beneath them. More than once in life I've had to say to myself, *I am not my feelings.*

Fours shouldn't worry about settling for having ordinary, medium-sized emotions. Regular feelings don't make Fours any less special, and once they get their emotional house in order, balancing highs and lows, they'll find they actually can form and hold on to relationships with others more easily. With prayer, meditation and self-knowledge, Fours' need to be unique will mellow. For Fours an important healing message is "We see you. You're beautiful. Don't be ashamed."

Have you ever seen the soft gaze that comes over a mother's face when she's looking into the eyes of her newborn? Fours need to remember this is how God looks at them. God sees, hears and understands them, and their identity can only be found in him. They should never settle for less.

TEN PATHS TO TRANSFORMATION FOR FOURS

1. Beware of self-absorption. Listen to others when they share stories about their own suffering, and realize it's not just you.

2. Watch out you don't instigate a drama or crisis with family or friends when your emotions start to feel run of the mill. All the world is *not* a stage, and you're not Shakespeare.

3. Go out of your way to find and express appreciation for what's present and unique in the people you love rather than always focusing on what's missing.

4. Offer yourself the gift of unconditional self-friendship as you work to unwind lifelong feelings of shame and inferiority. Never give up on yourself!

5. Don't wallow in suffering, but figure out what's causing it and do what you can to heal it.

6. Keep an eye out for envy! You never come out ahead when you compare yourself to other people.

7. Stop fantasizing about the ideal relationship, career or community and getting stuck in longing for it. Instead, work hard for what's possible and see it through to completion.

8. Don't look for beauty and meaning only in the extraordinary or unusual but in the ordinary and simple as well.

9. When the past calls, let it go to voicemail. It has nothing new to say to you.

10. Don't embellish and get swept up in your feelings. In the words of Jack Kornfield, "No emotion is final."

WHAT IT'S LIKE TO BE A FIVE

1. I can take care of myself, and I think others could do the same.

2. I don't always say things out loud, but in my head I am pretty sarcastic and cynical.

3. I often feel awkward around other people.

4. I'm okay if people ask me a few specific questions about myself, but I don't like it when people want too much information.

5. I need time alone.

6. If I want people to know how I feel I will tell them. I generally wish they wouldn't ask.

7. I think thoughts are more reliable than feelings.

8. I need a couple of days to process an experience or know how I feel about something.

9. People are wasteful. I hold on to what I have.

10. Often I find that I would rather observe than participate.

11. I trust myself. That means I think about things for a while and then I make my own decisions.

12. I can't understand why people get together to "just hang out."

13. I'm a listener.

14. I have to be very careful with my time and energy.

15. I get tired when I have to be with people for too long.

16. I often felt invisible as a child. Sometimes as an adult I choose to be invisible.

17. Sometimes I think I should be more generous. It's hard for me.

18. In groups, being uninformed makes me very uncomfortable.

19. I don't like big social gatherings. I'd rather be with a few people.

20. Material possessions don't make me happy.

9

TYPE FIVE

THE INVESTIGATOR

I think I am, therefore, I am. I think.

GEORGE CARLIN

Healthy Fives have a long view of things. They manage an appropriate balance between participation and observation, engaging with others comfortably and demonstrating true neutrality. These Fives are likely to have depth in knowledge in several areas of their lives, and they willingly share their findings with others. They live in a world of abundance, seeing themselves as part of the whole environment instead of separate from everyone and everything.

Average Fives hold to a scarcity mentality, which leads to hoarding time, space and affection. They feel more at home observing rather than participating in the external world, and thinking substitutes for feeling. Fives in this space tend to rely on themselves rather than faith, and they carefully measure how much time they spend with others. They struggle with anything that makes them feel incompetent or incapable.

Unhealthy Fives don't want to depend on anyone for anything. They have a defensive personality that is preoccupied with security, independence and privacy. These Fives are trapped in believing there is not enough and often express that way of thinking with judgment, cynicism and sarcasm. When they do participate in family or social gatherings, they stay separate from others.

Bill and I met and became fast friends in seminary. He was a psychiatrist who had decided to leave behind a thriving practice to pursue a doctorate in theology. We shared a love for Flannery O'Connor, Willie Nelson and G. K. Chesterton, and we spent hours hiking, playing squash and fly fishing together. Thankfully our wives became close friends too, so they were company for each other whenever Bill and I headed off to the mountains.

Bill was the most brilliant person I'd ever met up to that point in my life. He had attended an Ivy League university where he majored in classics, graduated first in his class from medical school and then spent two years in Switzerland studying Jungian psychoanalysis. He was a man who seemed to know more than the average savant about a wide range of subjects like art, philosophy, ancient history and architecture—not to mention he could read Homer's *Odyssey* in Greek.

Once while ordering lunch at a Mexican restaurant Bill broke into conversation with the waiter in Spanish. I'm not talking *"¿Dónde está el baño?"*–level Spanish; I mean "I hear Gabriel Garcia Marquez's new novel is quite good. Have you read it?"–level Spanish. You could bring up any obscure topic and somehow Bill knew at least a little something about it. He probably should have backed up some of the information sloshing around in his head to one of those secure servers you hear about in the Utah desert.

During our final semester Bill and I had a conversation during which he mentioned an upcoming trip to visit his sister who suffered from a serious lifelong illness. I was stunned. I had no idea Bill even had a sister, let alone that she was ill. In the days that followed I thought about our friendship, and it gradually dawned on me that there was a lot I didn't know about Bill. We'd spent hours hiking and fishing the Roaring Fork together, and in all that time he'd shared only a fraction of what I had told him about my own history, struggles, joys and disappointments. Fascinated to know about other people's lives and a great listener, Bill always found a way to shift the focus of conversation back to me whenever I asked him about his own life.

At the time I wasn't familiar with the Enneagram and didn't know that withholding personal information is a classic trait of Fives.

THE FIVE'S DEADLY SIN

Fives like Bill experience the world as intrusive, overwhelming and draining. It's a place where demand always outpaces supply. It asks for more than they want or think they have to give. Typically introverted and analytical, Fives don't believe they have enough inner resources or energy to meet the demands of life. They feel drained by prolonged involvement with other people or by having too many expectations placed on them. Every handshake, phone call, business meeting, social gathering or unexpected encounter seems to cost them more than it does other people. Fearful they don't have sufficient inner resources to function in the world, they detach and withdraw into the mind, where they feel more at home and confident. They monitor the amount of time they spend with others and hightail it back to the realm of the mind whenever possible to refuel.

We don't hear the word *avarice* very often, but avarice is the deadly sin of Fives. Typically we think of it as a greedy craving for money or material gain, but in Enneagram-speak it refers more to the Five's need to retain, a desire to clench and protect what little they already have rather than a desire to acquire more. Afraid there won't be enough, Fives pare down their needs and hoard the barest essentials to ensure they can maintain a self-sufficient existence now and in the future. For Fives this not only includes withholding their many resources but their time, energy, physical space, personal information, solitude and privacy as well. Fives value autonomy and self-containment, so they stockpile these things because they never want to be put in a position where they have to depend on others to take care of them. The idea of losing their independence and self-reliance terrifies them. Needless to say, Fives are reluctant to share their prized necessities with others.

Avarice also expresses itself in the Five's excessive desire for acquiring knowledge, information, ideas, conceptual models, expertise, interesting facts and understanding for how things work. Fives look to knowledge to provide them with what most people find through relationships, such as love, comfort and support.

Fives, Sixes and Sevens make up the Fear or Thinking Triad (also called the Fear or Head Triad), and each number has a distinct strategy for finding a sense of control and safe refuge in this unpredictable world. Fives are motivated by a desire to understand. To them, gathering knowledge and mastering information are not just interesting endeavors but keys to survival. By embarking on a lifelong quest for information, often about unusual or challenging subjects, Fives believe they can insulate themselves from emotional and spiritual harm. Albert Einstein, Oliver Sacks and director David Lynch are but a few examples of Fives who departed from well-worn paths to pioneer ideas and explore subjects few others have. What better way to build self-esteem (and sometimes feel superior to others) and insulate yourself from others than to become an expert in a niche field of study?

FAMOUS FIVES

Stephen Hawking
Dietrich Bonhoeffer
Bill Gates

Fives are minimalists. They don't need or want too many things. In their minds, the more possessions people have, the more energy they'll have to expend thinking about them, maintaining them or restocking them. Unfortunately, Fives' desire to keep life simple and economical can reveal itself in their appearance. They don't win fashion shows.

In the end avarice catches up to Fives. They hoard too much, emotionally speaking. Their greed for privacy and their fear of self-disclosure lead to isolation. Believing the old maxim "He who has the knowledge has the power," they prefer to keep too much knowledge and those few necessities to themselves. Even worse, they scrimp on love and affection and stingily withhold it from the people who most want to support and care for them.

ALL ABOUT FIVES OR INVESTIGATORS

Fives can be a bit difficult to get to know, but they do share some general characteristics that mark them as a tribe.

Fives prefer to observe. Fives can appear to be loners, and sometimes they are. They often strike people as emotionally distant, not entirely present or at home in their bodies, aloof and sometimes intellectually arrogant. In part this is because Fives *observe life from a distance rather than jumping in and participating* in it. Watching from the sidelines, along with obtaining knowledge, is their first line of defense. If they can observe and understand what's happening maybe they'll feel in the loop or be prepared should something suddenly be expected of them. Not all Fives are smart, but they're all observant. You might glimpse them at a party observing the crowd from the periphery or circling a social event like an anthropologist performing work in the field, collecting and analyzing information on people and the general goings-on. This tendency to observe is not passive, however; far from it. Fives are *actively* watching—taking in information and filing it for future use.

Despite their tendency toward observation, many Fives are social. Some especially enjoy being with fellow knowledge lovers, the intellectually curious, or those who share their enthusiasm for a niche subject or hobby, such as rare book manuscripts, German opera or perhaps collecting *Star Trek* paraphernalia.

One benefit of all this observation from the periphery is that Fives can remain objective even if they have a dog in other people's fights. When it comes to being neutral, Fives are like Switzerland. If I'm faced with a major life decision and my feelings are clouding my judgment, I call my friend Chris. As a Five he can sort through the facts, study the situation from every angle and then present me with a well-reasoned, unbiased case for why he thinks I should choose a particular course of action, even if it's not what I want to hear or might somehow negatively affect his life. And because Fives are capable of being neutral, they rarely react; rather, they respond. When stewarded properly, this is an amazing gift. (Like Nines, Fives are able to see both sides to things, but because they're not worried about causing conflict they'll shoot straight up with you.)

Fives collect knowledge. Knowledge and information of almost any kind (even the strangest information) provide Fives with a sense of control and a defense against feelings of inadequacy. Fives also collect information or knowledge because

> "Understanding is a kind of ecstasy."
> **CARL SAGAN**

they don't want to appear foolish or uninformed, or be humiliated for not having the correct answer. They don't want to feel incapable or inept, which is what they believe they are. Needless to say, the best and worst thing that ever happened to Fives is the advent of the Internet. Once they tumble down that bottomless wormhole, these information junkies fall into their trance of knowledge collecting and there's no telling when they're coming back and what new and fun information they're hauling back with them. I saw this in action when one afternoon I called to check in on my friend Bill.

"My printer broke and I've been on the Internet trying to figure out how to fix it," he said.

"Bill, how long have you been working on this?" I asked, sighing.

"Since 8:00 a.m.," he admitted.

I looked at my watch. "It's 5:00 p.m.! Did you think to take the printer back to where you bought it and have them repair it?"

There was a long pause.

"It's an old Inkjet. They stopped making parts for it years ago," he said, sheepishly.

"You're a $200-an-hour psychiatrist and you just wasted an entire day reading up on how to repair a printer you couldn't give away at a yard sale?" There was a pause.

"Yes, but now I know the history of printing beginning with the Gutenberg press to the present day," he said triumphantly.

As humorous as that story may be, Fives really do end up as roadkill on the information highway. For Fives, computers and the Internet provide another way to avoid interaction with people—which is the last thing they need.

Compartmentalization and privacy. Compartmentalization is a signature defense mechanism against feeling overwhelmed in the life of a Five. Believing their inner resources are limited and seeking to feel in control, Fives assign their job, marriage, hobbies, friendships and other commitments to separate mental cubbyholes. This way they can determine precisely how much energy each will require to maintain, apportion it correctly and deal with one compartment at a time. Soon they discover life will not cooperate with their desire to keep the different areas of their lives partitioned off

> "I cannot live without brain-work. What else is there to live for?"
>
> **SHERLOCK HOLMES**

from each other. Similarly, Fives maintain friendships in each compartment with people who neither meet nor know about each other. A few years ago I arrived at the funeral of my Five friend Sam, and to my amazement the church was packed. Unable to find a seat, I stood at the back and wondered whether I'd stumbled into the wrong service. Apart from three or four people, I hardly knew anyone there, despite the fact that for ten years Sam and I had been part of the same men's Bible study and hung out together regularly.

At the post-service reception I learned some of the mourners were members of an astronomy club Sam had been active in for a long time. Several others were fellow crew members from a boat he raced on. I met five guys he biked with on Saturday mornings, and a bunch of bird watchers who had flown in from Baja, California.

Astronomy? Blue-footed boobies? Who was this guy?

To maintain their privacy, Fives tell each group of friends or colleagues one part of their story, but they never tell any group their whole story. They won't tell you about every activity they're involved in or introduce you to the friends they've made in their different spheres. As a young Five once jokingly told Suzanne, "I'm terrified I will wake up from a coma one day and the people standing around my bed will be from all the different parts of my life. What if I don't know how long I've been unconscious and what they've told one another?"

Fives aren't ruled by their feelings. Of all types Fives are the most emotionally detached. This doesn't mean Fives don't have emotions, but that they want to have control over unpredictable feelings that might threaten to overwhelm them. For Fives, detachment means they can have an emotion and then let it go. Then they have the next emotion, and then let it go. Fives fancy themselves rational thinkers and see the rest of us as being irrational. In particular, they look at feeling-centered types like Twos, Threes and Fours and wonder how they can possibly waste so much energy on all that inner turmoil.

I'm a Four. When it comes to feelings I'm flypaper. I've had feelings show up and stick around so long I should've charged them rent. At seminary if I became worked up over something I would go to Bill, who listened patiently to me. If I became emotionally incontinent, however, he would move from looking concerned to regarding me with all the warmth of a snow owl, blinking and staring at me as if to say, "When does this end?"

Fives need to have time to process emotions. At Enneagram gatherings people will hear their number described and become emotional because they finally feel understood (or, on the flip side, embarrassed and exposed). Not so with Fives. They take in all the information and don't feel anything until they have a few days on their own to process it *in private*. For them life is like a knowledge salad bar. They get in line, pick what they want, then bag it up, take it home, eat it and over the next week digest it. They need extended periods of time alone where they can process their thoughts and feelings.

> "I'd like to be the kind of person who can enjoy things at the time, instead of having to go back in my head and enjoy them."
>
> *DAVID FOSTER WALLACE*

This delay can bewilder people of other types. When Bill and I went to see the movie *Philadelphia* years ago, I responded like a typical Four. When the lights came on at the end of the film I sobbed like a baby. I was all but looking for a grief counselor in the lobby, while Bill gave me that signature snow owl stare. At the time I thought he was a little heartless, but now I know Bill had to go home where he could try to think his way to his feelings.

FIVES AS CHILDREN

Many Fives I know say they grew up with a parent who was intrusive or engulfing, while others describe childhoods that lacked affection or deep, meaningful interactions with their caretakers. Sensitive and quiet, these Five kids took refuge in the realm of their minds where they could fend off or hide from an overbearing parent, as well as work through their feelings out of sight.

As kids, Fives are curious, imaginative and comfortable being alone. Many are computer whizzes and voracious readers who enjoy collecting things. My Five friend Dan grew up with six rowdy siblings in a tiny house in rural Texas. To escape the mayhem he turned one-half of his father's tool shed into a haven.

"I spent a million hours in that shed reading *The Lord of the Rings* and taking things apart to figure out how they worked. It was where my friends and I made our first foray into the world of computer coding. My brothers and sisters were loud, outgoing attention seekers, while I didn't ask for much really. I couldn't have faulted my mother if one night over dinner she had looked up from her plate at me and said, 'Wait, who are you?'"

Kids who are Fives are usually quiet and self-contained. They are uncomfortable when they can't take care of themselves, so they have learned to hold on to themselves instead of others. They find answers to most of their questions within themselves, and they have far more information about things than they share.

These kids have mixed feelings about school. They are smart and enjoy learning, and they usually make good grades. However, the social demands of school are hard to read and a challenge to accommodate. It feels to them like people either want too much time with them or not enough. They are comfortable spending time alone so they would be content with just one or two friends, but they aren't adept at sharing feelings, and their need for personal space is difficult for other kids to understand.

These thoughtful kids have significant fears, so they often appear to be more serious than they are. They have to be invited to be playful, and even then it feels a bit frivolous and awkward. Deep down, they are tender and compassionate and would like to be more open with their love and affection, but the vulnerability they feel is too much to navigate.

We all pick up wounding messages as kids. If you're a Five, come up with words to articulate the wounding message you picked up; it will probably be some variation on the broad themes of competency and connection, like "You're not capable of handling the demands of life and relationships. To survive you'll need to emotionally detach and hide."

FIVES IN RELATIONSHIPS

When it comes to relationships, Fives may be the most misunderstood of all types. It's important to remember just how taxing social engagement can be for them. For example, Anne and I have a Five friend named Georgia who is a private tutor for children with profound learning disabilities. Quiet and kind, Georgia can only take so much social interaction before her tank empties and she has to go home to recharge. At large gatherings she and her husband, an outgoing Seven, will often drive two cars, as she almost always wants to leave before he does. At our weekly small group supper club Georgia often clears the table and withdraws to the kitchen to wash the dishes while the rest of us continue talking. It's Georgia's way, and we've learned not to insist she stay and socialize. Georgia isn't cold, but connecting with her can be challenging. Like all Fives her talk style is presentational or lecture; if you ask her what she feels, she'll tell you what she thinks. Fives have tall, thick boundaries. It's as if Georgia's on the other side of a three-lane highway and you have to yell over traffic to establish a real connection with her.

Fives don't want to be sucked into your emotional dramas, which is another relational challenge for them. They aren't cold-hearted jerks; on the contrary, they will listen and be supportive while you talk about your feelings. But they don't want to be made to feel responsible for those feelings. They'll take responsibility for their own emotions, and they expect you to take responsibility for yours.

Fives have to have independence. People who are in a relationship with them need to understand that this is not a preference but a necessity. Because Fives want to maintain their independence and self-sufficiency, you might wake up one Saturday morning to find your Five spouse has taken the dogs and headed off somewhere without leaving a note telling you where they have gone or when they plan to return. When they surface several hours later you might have to ask them where they went or else it might not occur to them to tell you.

People in a relationship with a Five have to recognize and honor the Five's need for privacy and times of solitude. At home Fives usually have a space where they can withdraw to recharge. A Five friend who is a huge audiophile built out a room in his basement where he goes to read, smoke cigars and listen to his collection of John Coltrane records. His wife calls it "the hermitage." For Fives on a tighter budget, their retreat might be a leather chair tucked away in a nook or a simple workbench in the basement. Often their special space is littered with books, papers, years of *National Geographic* magazines and odd curios picked up while traveling. But this is *their* space and *their* mess, and it's unlikely a Five will express appreciation if you trespass on it without a very good reason.

The high value Fives place on privacy also extends to keeping their cards close to the vest. Though Fives want to get together or be included, they rarely initiate social interactions, so I was surprised when my friend Adam called at the last minute to ask whether I wanted to join him for dinner.

"If it were any other night I'd love to get together, but tonight is Anne's birthday and the kids and I are surprising her by taking her to that great Italian place she loves over on 12 South," I explained.

"Okay," he said. "Some other time." And he hung up.

Later I contemplated what would have happened if our roles had been reversed. What would Adam have said if I had called to ask if he wanted to join me for dinner, but he had a conflict?

He'd say, "I can't." Full stop. He wouldn't tell me why he couldn't go—where he was going instead, what he was doing or who he was doing it with. That's private. He would provide only the facts I needed to know and no more. By comparison, I shared "insider information" about my family's plans. I even gave him the restaurant's dang address. Fives may not be aware of it, but when people share these trivial life details it's a way of leaving a door open for the other person to talk about what's happening in their life. Adam might have said, "How are the kids? Does Anne still enjoy her job? I contracted food poisoning from the calamari at that restaurant, so don't order it." This may sound like mundane stuff, but disclosing even little things about our lives is like Miracle-Gro for relationships. By keeping everyone on a need-to-know basis, Fives can make their friends and even their partners wonder, "Do I really know this person? Will I *ever* know this person?" Like flowers, relationships don't grow in the dark. Relationships bloom in the light of self-disclosure.

Spouses of Fives sometimes tell Suzanne and me they feel emotionally neglected. The husband of a Five once told me, "My wife and I have been married for thirty years and adore each other, but she's so independent and mentally self-sustaining that I know she could adjust to life without me better than I could without her. It's taken time for me to be okay knowing she doesn't need me as much, or at least in the same way, as I need her."

Fives need and enjoy being with other people, but don't ask them if they'd like to "hang out." A Five wants a reason for getting together like a birthday party, a movie or to go with you to an antique car show, a subject about which they have no knowledge—yet. But if the agenda is just hanging out, they'd rather do that alone.

To further understand Fives, let's use a car analogy. Imagine you have a tank in which you keep all the fuel you need to interact with people all day. Fives have smaller tanks than other numbers, so as the day goes on they're checking that gauge more often and becoming increasingly aware that they're running out of fuel and need to get home.

There are also amazing benefits to being in relationships with Fives. They're not emotionally needy, don't have impossible expectations of the people they love and typically stay calm when the folks around them are all falling apart. You can also share your darkest secrets with Fives and know they will hold them in sacred trust. Like a priest, they will keep whatever you tell them under the "seal of the confessional," in part because they know how important such confidentiality would be to them if the shoe were on the other foot.

Fives won't often tell you they love you, but this doesn't mean they don't. I spend sixty days a year speaking at retreats and conferences. One or two times a year Bill will visit my website to check my calendar and ask whether he can meet me where I'm speaking, even if it involves his having to get on a plane and he's already heard me give the talk before. That's love, people.

Love is dangerous and demanding. For a relationship to flourish, two people have to openly share not only their thoughts but also their feelings, which is a challenge for Fives. It requires them to share space, exert less control over the time they have alone, sacrifice privacy, and cope with another person's overwhelming emotions. To make it work, they have to give up a large measure of the security, independence and privacy that's held their life together since they were children. Their partners

> "A good marriage is one in which each partner appoints the other to be the guardian of his solitude, and thus they show each other the greatest possible trust."
>
> *RAINER MARIA RILKE*

and friends can help them by being patient while Fives learn to identify and express their feelings. It's no small thing when a Five takes the risk of exchanging secrets and commits to walk beside another person. Celebrate it every day if a Five has chosen to undertake this journey with you. Chances are you are more special than you know.

FIVES AT WORK

In the professional world Fives are valued for their cool, clear, pioneering, analytical minds. From Microsoft founder Bill Gates to novelist Jean Paul Sartre, from physicist Stephen Hawking to primatologist Jane Goodall, Fives are well represented on any list of the world's greatest innovators and thinkers.

Not every Five can be a titan of industry or a Nobel Prize winner, so they may choose careers as engineers, scientific researchers, librarians, professors, computer programmers or psychologists. Because they remain calm in a crisis, they make great emergency room doctors and EMTs. Because they're masters of observation, Fives can evolve into magnificent artists. Author Joan Didion, painter Georgia O'Keefe, lead singer of Radiohead Thom Yorke and actor Anthony Hopkins are but a few of the Fives whose artistic vision has left a mark on the world.

Regardless of what they do or how successful they are, what Fives need most at work is predictability. If Fives know what demands will be placed on them every day, they'll know how to wisely apportion their inner resources so they'll make it home without running out of gas.

To this end, Fives don't like meetings. If they have no choice but to attend one, they will want to know precisely when it begins and ends, who else will be there, and what the agenda is going to be. When a meeting is finished Fives are eager to go, so if the person leading it asks if anyone has any last questions and someone's hand shoots up in the air, Fives will bury their face in their hands and mutter, "Give me a letter opener and this will all be over in a flash."

In leadership positions, Fives can overfocus on a project and end up not supporting or paying enough attention to other people. To maintain privacy and to guard their inner resources, they set up lines of defense between themselves and others. They'll gladly surrender their prestigious corner office with the glass walls to an image-conscious Three colleague and seek out another spot where people will have trouble finding them—like in the basement, since they hate to be interrupted while they're working. If they're high enough on the corporate ladder they will have an administrative assistant and a few interns who will run interference and insulate them from having to meet or talk to too many people.

Fives would rather you give them a project, tell them when it's due, and allow them to accomplish it however and wherever they choose. Many of the traditional rewards for excellence at work aren't primary motivators for Fives, who aren't typically materialistic and aren't always angling, like Threes can be, for a promotion or a raise. If you want to recognize and reward Fives for a job well done, give them more autonomy. Independence is what they crave, even when they're working on a team. They are generally impatient with group decisions because they don't like long discussions or having to listen to people free-associate ideas.

Fives can successfully hold positions that require making presentations or making speeches, so long as they have time to prepare. They don't like to be unexpectedly put on the spot or asked to spontaneously say or do something. If Fives know what's expected of them and they're kept well informed about what's happening, they perform great.

WINGS

Fives are wedged between the passionate, intense Four on the one side and the loyal but anxious Six on the other. Either or both the qualities of those types can be available to the Five.

Fives with a Four wing (5w4). These Fives are more creative, sensitive, empathetic and self-absorbed than 5w6s. Independent and often eccentric, 5w4s are not sure what to do with their feelings but would rather process them alone than in a group. Think actor Robert De Niro, photographer Annie Leibovitz or physicist Albert Einstein. Not bad company.

Fives with a Four wing are more likely to experience melancholy. The connection to Four's energy and depth of emotion helps these Fives be more tender with themselves and less emotionally guarded around others. Healthy 5w4s are able to communicate their own feelings to the people they love.

Five with a Six wing (5w6). Fear plays a more prominent role in the life of a 5w6 than in the life of a 5w4. They are more anxious, cautious and skeptical, but they're also more social and loyal than 5w4. Fives with six wings live more in their minds and will question authority and the status quo.

Fives with a Six wing are also more relational. With a Six influence Fives are more aware of their own fear, which increases their interest in forming alliances with others in the various communities they are a part of. They are often socially awkward, and they remain skeptical of others, but getting to know people is more comforting than disconcerting.

STRESS AND SECURITY

Stress. In stress Fives instinctually move to the not-so-healthy side of Seven, where they will hoard and cling more tightly to things, which only makes their world feel smaller and smaller. When this happens they turn their attention away from the needs of others and focus almost solely on their own need for safety and independence.

Here also Fives become frivolous, disorganized and distracted to the point of not being able to complete tasks. They're still living in their heads, but they stop short of thinking through the consequences of their behavior. In this space Fives can become rude, condescending and disconnected.

Security. When Fives feel secure they move toward the positive side of Eight, which is a gigantic move! When this happens Fives become infinitely more spontaneous, outspoken and physically present. The difference is so striking people will say, "What's gotten into Holly? She's suddenly so energetic, confident and talkative." Fives who want to know and experience life abundant without it costing them more than they can afford to lose can achieve that on the high side of Eight.

SPIRITUAL TRANSFORMATION

When it comes to spiritual work, Fives have an advantage over the rest of us. They don't cling to their ego with as tight a grip. Their love for solitude makes them natural contemplatives. They are attracted to simplicity, forming fewer attachments to worldly things and letting go more readily when they do. People of other numbers who are on the road to spiritual transformation might envy the Five's inner calm and detachment.

When they exaggerate it, however, detachment ceases to be a virtue. For Fives it risks devolving into disconnection from their feelings to prevent injury and depletion. It makes them cold, aloof and relationally unavailable—observers rather than participants in life. From a Christian perspective that's not detachment. "The ultimate goal of detachment is engagement," writes David Benner. "We detach so we can re-order our attachments and then, aligned and cooperating with the inflow of Grace into our deepest self, we can allow love to pass through us to touch and heal others in the world." To mature spiritually, Fives will need to learn this pattern of detaching in order to engage.

Fives need to practice connecting to their emotions in real time. A person can't celebrate Christmas on Monday and not feel it until Friday! If everything I've said in this chapter until now makes Fives feel miserable, I encourage them to feel that misery now, not next month. Once they master first attaching to feelings and then letting them go, they can teach others how to do it, because the rest of us get entangled in our feelings way too much.

Fives who seek to be free of their default patterns should recognize how often their actions are driven by fear. Like Sixes and Sevens, Fives' deadly sin is fear, and they're motivated by a desire for security. Aware that they have limited resources, they wonder how much information, how much affection, how much energy, how much privacy, how much money, how much *anything* they can afford to give away and how much they should conserve for themselves.

How different would Fives' lives be if they embraced a mindset of abundance? This mentality says that when we give, we receive. This is the algebra of the gospel. What if Fives trusted that there was more than enough to go around in life, so they could give more away?

To some extent, Fives also have to become comfortable with dependence, or at least interdependence. Fives have been motivated to live so self-sufficiently that they never have to depend on anyone else. Yet there is a humility that comes when we allow other people to take care of us. For Fives, establishing so many boundaries that they never have to experience depending on anyone else sets them up for a great loss. It also deprives those who love them of the joy of caring for them.

TEN PATHS TO TRANSFORMATION FOR FIVES

1. Allow your feelings to arise naturally and experience them in the present moment, and then you can let them go.

2. Recognize when you're succumbing to a scarcity mentality by hoarding affection, privacy, knowledge, time, love, money, material possessions or thoughts.

3. When something occurs that seems to elicit emotions in other people, try to feel with them in the moment rather than saving those feelings to process later.

4. Try sharing more of your life with others, trusting they won't misuse that information.

5. Venture out of your comfort zone and share more of who you are and what you have with others.

6. Try to remember that you don't have to have the answers for everything. You won't look foolish, just human.

7. Call a friend and offer to hang out, for no reason at all other than to enjoy each other's company.

8. Allow yourself some material and experiential luxuries. Buy a new mattress! Travel!

9. Take up yoga or another activity that will connect you with your body. Overcoming the disconnect between your body and head will be life changing.

10. Even when you're unsure of yourself, jump into a conversation rather than withdrawing from it.

WHAT IT'S LIKE TO BE A SIX

1. I'm always imagining and planning for the worst.

2. I often don't trust people who are in authority.

3. People say I am loyal, understanding, funny and compassionate.

4. Most of my friends don't have as much anxiety as I do.

5. I act quickly in a crisis, but when things settle down I fall apart.

6. When my partner and I are doing really well in our relationship I find myself wondering what will happen to spoil it.

7. Being sure I've made the right decision is almost impossible.

8. I'm aware that fear has dictated many of my choices in life.

9. I don't like to find myself in unpredictable situations.

10. I find it hard to stop thinking about the things I'm worried about.

11. I'm generally not comfortable with extremes.

12. I usually have so much to do it's hard for me to finish tasks.

13. I'm most comfortable when I'm around people who are pretty much like me.

14. People tell me I can be overly pessimistic.

15. I am slow to start, and once I do get started I find myself continuing to think about what could go wrong.

16. I don't trust people who give me too many compliments.

17. It helps me to have things in some kind of order.

18. I like to be told I am good at my job, but I get very nervous when my boss wants to add to my responsibilities.

19. I have to know people for a long time before I can really trust them.

20. I am skeptical of things that are new and unknown.

10

TYPE SIX

THE LOYALIST

There's no harm in hoping for the best as long
as you're prepared for the worst.

STEPHEN KING

Healthy Sixes have learned to trust their own experiences of life. They are aware that certainty and accurate predictability are not likely in most situations. They are productive, logical thinkers who almost always organize their thoughts and actions around what would be most advantageous for the common good. Loyal, honest and reliable, healthy Sixes are clear-eyed judges of character. These Sixes have come to believe that in the end everything will be all right.

Average Sixes question almost everything. They struggle to get out of their heads and the pattern of worst-case-scenario planning. They are overly focused on authority and can be either subservient on the one hand or rebellious on the other. They find the world to be an unsafe place, and they respond with fight or flight. These Sixes, while managing all of their anxiety, are committed to education, church, government, family and social service organizations.

Unhealthy Sixes find danger around every corner. Their anxiety borders on paranoia, as they fear that the world is unfair and that most people are not who they say they are and cannot be trusted. Unable to trust themselves either, they look to authority figures and experts to make decisions on their behalf. These Sixes find fault in others and tend to fall into patterns associated with the mental mechanism of projection.

In 1999, authors Joshua Piven and David Borgenicht released *The Worst-Case Scenario Survival Handbook.* Providing humorous but real-life instructions for what to do in unusually dire circumstances, the book advertised itself as "the essential companion for a perilous age." Both frightening and funny, it offered pithy chapters on how to perform a tracheotomy, identify a bomb, land a plane, survive if your parachute fails to open, deal with a charging bull, jump from a building into a dumpster and escape from killer bees, among other things.

Someone gave me a copy of *The Worst-Case Scenario Survival Handbook* when it came out. I shrugged and said, "Meh."

It sold ten million copies.

To whom should the now unfathomably rich and grateful authors send a thank-you note for spearheading their book's epic sales? They could start with Enneagram Sixes, who probably account for half those sales.

Sixes see a dangerous world in which disaster can strike at any moment. Appearances are deceiving. People have hidden agendas. They keep their eyes peeled for possible threats and mentally rehearse what they will do when the worst happens. For Sixes, imagining and planning for potential catastrophes is a way of maintaining a sense of safety, control and certainty in an unpredictable world. Given their penchant for constantly asking "What if . . . ?" or "What will I do when . . . ?" I can't fathom a Six seeing a book describing itself as a "guide for surviving life's sudden turns for the worse" and not buying two copies—the first to read and the second as a backup in the event someone steals the first one.

The more I know about life and people, the more I love and appreciate Sixes. Called Loyalists, Sixes are the most faithful and dependable people on the Enneagram. (Sixes are also sometimes called the Devil's Advocate, the Questioner, the Skeptic, the Trooper or the Guardian.) They keep a watchful eye over us. They safeguard our values. They're the glue that holds the world together. Many Enneagram teachers believe these reliable, warm, funny and self-sacrificing people make up more than half the world's population. That our cities and towns are teeming with these steadfast and vigilant citizens should have a tonic effect on us.

THE SIX'S DEADLY SIN

By now you know what's coming, right? Sixes are wonderful, but they too have a shadow side they need to guard against. Sixes' deadly sin is *fear*, and they suffer a deep-seated need to feel secure.

Though we say fear is the sin toward which the Six gravitates, what Sixes actually experience is anxiety. Fear is what arises when you're in the presence of a clear and immediate source of danger—like when a guy wearing a hockey goalie's mask kicks your door down and chases you around your apartment while wielding a chainsaw over his head. Anxiety, by contrast, is a vague, free-floating sense of apprehension that arises in response to an unknown or potential threat that may never materialize. It's what you feel when you *imagine* what would happen if a guy wearing a hockey goalie's mask ever chased you around your apartment with a chainsaw. Fear says, "Something wrong is actually happening!" while anxiety is more anticipatory: "What if this happened or that happened? What if . . . What if . . . What if . . . ?" That's the campaign slogan.

Sixes even experience elevated anxiety when life is going smoothly because they wonder what might come along and ruin it. The relationships or jobs that seem stable today might evaporate or be taken away tomorrow. In the words of Steven Wright, "If everything seems to be going well, you have obviously overlooked something."

My childhood was populated with anxious Sixes.

My first-grade teacher, Sr. Mary Elizabeth (may perpetual light shine upon her), was a Six for sure. At least once a day she'd take a break from the lesson plan and ask a random tenebrous question like, "Children, what would you do if someone held a gun to your head and forced you to decide between denying your faith and death?" If you asked a group of seven-year-olds questions like that today, someone would call Child Protective Services.

Sr. Mary Elizabeth wasn't the only person in my life pondering those questions. Growing up my siblings and I had a nanny who appeared to suffer from pretraumatic stress disorder. She wore herself out with worry about what could happen to us. Don't run with scissors, you'll stab your sister. Don't eat food from a can with dents, you'll die of salmonella. You'll get electrocuted if you take a shower in a thunderstorm. If you stand too close to the microwave, you'll turn out like your cousin Marty. To thwart would-be carjackers she made us roll up our windows and lock our car doors when we drove through "rough" areas of town. I grew up in Greenwich, Connecticut, a town where people think "bad taste" is a crime you should worry about, not carjacking.

FAMOUS SIXES

Ellen DeGeneres
Jon Stewart
Frodo Baggins

All humor aside, the Six's deadly sin of fear is very real, and it has serious implications.

These are difficult times for Sixes. The air we breathe is humid with anxiety. Regrettably, you and I are not the first to figure out that 3.5 billion of our planet's full-time residents (plus or minus a few hundred million) are easily motivated by fear and a deep need for security and certainty. Politicians, cable news anchors, marketing experts, highhanded preachers and other unprincipled grifters know it as well. To win votes, hike viewership, raise money and sell home-security systems, these panic-mongering demagogues, pundits and advertising execs deliberately use well-researched scare tactics to prey on all of us, but they target folks like Sixes in particular. We all need to learn how to prevent fear from taking over our lives, but Sixes especially do. History demonstrates that when anxious folks make decisions as a group based on fear and a frustrated desire for security, bad things can happen.

ALL ABOUT SIXES OR LOYALISTS

Sixes have a strong need for security and consistency. They appreciate order, plans and rules. They like the comfort and predictability that clear laws and guidelines offer us. Like Ones, they'll call Ikea's 1-800 number to order an unnecessary bolt for their new dining room table, not because it won't be perfect but because they can visualize the holiday table collapsing, the ambulance coming to whisk Grandpa to the hospital with a broken leg and third-degree gravy burns, and so on, ad infinitum.

Sixes value community. They won't leave a church if they're not "being fed," the announcements are too long, the church has gotten too big (or too small), the music is (fill in the blank), or they don't agree with everything the pastor says from the pulpit. Sixes are the most loyal number on the Enneagram. They are devoted group members who, once they commit to a community, put down stakes and won't abandon it over small matters of disagreement.

Though they are typically wary and skeptical of people at first, once you've won Sixes' trust they're with you for life. Sixes want to feel connected to the people they love. These are the mothers who call every day to "check in," wanting to know what you're doing and that you're safe. Sixes have a remarkable ability to bond us together. They believe in the importance of family, home, raising responsible children, and marriage, and they make choices based on their values, in part because they have very high security needs.

Sixes are full of doubts and questions. When it comes time to make decisions they become like the worry-prone *Star Wars* protocol droid C-3PO: "We're doomed!" Suffering from analysis paralysis, they turn to friends, coworkers, family members and experts for advice because they don't trust their own thinking. They make up their mind then change it again. They feel pulled one way, then pushed in another. They waffle and equivocate, driving themselves and others crazy as they swing back and forth between yay, nay and maybe. In the words of St. James, they are the ones who, because they doubt, are "like a wave of the sea, carried forward by the wind one moment and driven back the next" (James 1:6 Phillips).

Part of the problem is Sixes see both sides to everything. If you're a Six reading this book right now you might be thinking, *Yes, I see your point but on the other hand . . .* or *Ian and Suzanne sound like they've thought a lot about this, but there's always a possibility that . . .* Sixes are surprised when they discover that other people aren't as fearful as they are, but they

> "I'm not afraid, but I'm very nervous."
> **JOHN IRVING**

identify right away with their ongoing battle with self-doubt and second-guessing themselves. When faced with decisions, Sixes freeze like deer transfixed by car headlights, paralyzed about which direction they should go.

There are two kinds of Sixes, each of whom manages fear, their need for security and their relationship to authority differently. One Six is very loyal and gives their full attention to authority because they think that's where security lies. Always loyal to authority, these Sixes seek to please and obey the rules. They are deferential to their bosses, trying their best to please because they view the authority as the source of their security. We call these folks *phobic Sixes*.

There's another kind of Six who also focuses on authority, only they're not nearly as agreeable or compliant. These folks are wary of authority figures. They keep a weather eye on those in charge in case they try to pull the wool over someone's eyes or pull a fast one. Called *counterphobic Sixes*, these folks will strike if they smell a rat. They seek security not by avoiding or placating a perceived threat but by deliberately provoking and attacking it. Their security comes from conquering the source of their fear, not capitulating to it.

In reality, most Sixes are a mixture of phobic and counterphobic, which reflects their vacillating, doubting temperament. The phobic Sixes fall back and flee while the counterphobic Sixes try to conquer or defeat whatever their fears are. Most Sixes bounce back and forth between these two poles. To borrow a phrase from Churchill, they are "either at your feet or at your throat." Whether Sixes are phobic or counter-phobic, the bottom line is fear, and the focus for all Sixes is authority.

SIXES AS CHILDREN

Kids who are Sixes learn to worry early. They're Velcro for messages like "Don't swim for thirty minutes after you eat or you'll get a cramp and drown" or "Never talk to strangers." Growing up I heard all manner of crazy warnings, but few stuck. But when these kids figure out the world isn't safe and the adults in charge can't always be trusted, they respond by obeying or rebelling. Wherever they go they know who is in charge, and keep their eyes dialed in on them.

These kids respond to life in a measured way. They'll watch one or two kids jump off a twenty-foot ledge into a lake before possibly doing it themselves. They're hesitant because kids who can't trust their environment find it hard to trust themselves. Kids who lack self-confidence typically have a difficult time receiving encouragement, so they miss out on the very messages that would make them more secure and help them to trust themselves at a deeper level.

Teachers and coaches love kids who are Sixes. They are good followers and listeners. Because they're loyal they hold groups of friends together. Only a few of them ever crave the spotlight, but they do want to be in the chorus. They like to be part of a group, so team sports and school activities are a win for them. They find a sense of comfort in routines that are predictable, and they grow up to be the folks who hold together all of the communities we all count on to make sense of our lives.

Many (not all) Six kids find themselves in unstable situations growing up. Because they are unable to trust their environment, they doubt themselves and look to other people for courage and advice. If they grow up with an alcoholic, for example, they learn never to let their guard down and to always assume the worst will happen so as not to be caught unawares.

My pal Lance's father would often fly into fits of rage. Every night he and his brother would look out their bedroom window to watch their dad get out of the car because they could tell what kind of mood he was in from how hard he slammed the car door. Like Lance, Six kids pick up small cues that a danger or threat is present, and stay safe by learning to predict whether someone is going to hurt them.

Sixes make terrific friends or partners when they're spiritually healthy and growing in self-knowledge. Loyal to a fault, Sixes mean it when they say, "Until death do us part." Quick-witted and charming, Loyalists can leverage their anxiety and be very funny. Sixes like Larry David can turn their exaggerated anxieties, insecurities and catastrophizing into fodder for self-deprecating stories that will keep their friends laughing for days. Listen to early recordings of Woody Allen stand-up routines if you want to hear a phobic Six who made his fortune airing his self-doubts, or a counterphobic Six George Carlin aggressively questioning everything and everyone.

SIXES IN RELATIONSHIPS

But Sixes' way of seeing the world through fear-tinted lenses can wreak havoc on their relationships. They're not easy to be with, particularly in the beginning of the relationship. People who need security and certainty will keep their guard up. They will try to guess what you're thinking. Afraid of being emotionally blindsided and having been hurt in the past, they will watch for hints of imminent betrayal or abandonment. A Six will pepper you with you questions like, "Are we still good?" or "What if you wake up one day and decide you don't love me anymore?" They will alternate between pushing you away and clinging to you. And because they're doubtful, Sixes will assume you too are doubtful, which leads them to question you. This doesn't exactly achieve what they're after— greater commitment and security—as such whining tends to drive loved ones further away.

It helps Sixes in the throes of doubt to remind them of your commitment to them. Never scold, dismiss or make fun of Sixes' doubts about their relationship with you unless you want to amp up their anxiety that it's not going to work out. Calm, reasoned reassurance is the key.

Even when Sixes begin to trust their relationship with you, there's still the rest of the dangerous, fickle world for them to contend with. At times it's hard to be with people who are always imagining and preparing for disasters. If only they could stop awfulizing and relax, right? When Sixes begin to get stuck in worst-case-scenario thinking, ask them to walk you step by step through the chain of negative events they see happening in it. At each step, stop and say, "You're right, that sounds bad. Then what would happen or who would be there to help you?" After a while, one of two things will occur. The plot of their nightmare scenario will either spiral into something so irrational as to be absurd and they'll start laughing, or they'll begin to see (often with your guidance) that as horrible as the feared future event would be, they would have the inner and outer resources to cope and thrive if it came to pass. Remember: worst-case-scenario thinking needs to be managed, not discounted. If you call them pessimists, they'll only argue back that they're realists.

Sixes are always going back and forth about things, and that can be exasperating in relationships. They decide, then second guess; they decide, then second guess. And just when you think they've finally made a decision, they'll wake you up in the middle of the night to say they've changed their minds. *Sigh.*

What's the source of all this waffling? They never learned to connect with and trust their inner guidance system. They often doubt their ability to make good decisions because, as a rule, they forget past successes. Sometimes those who love them need to remind them how well things turned out the last time they made a decision and stuck to it, or how they made it through if the results were less than they'd hoped. No one bats one thousand in this life.

> "Anxiety is like a rocking chair. It gives you something to do, but it doesn't get you very far."
>
> *JODI PICOULT*

The wonderful news about Sixes in relationships is they're troopers. With time and reassurance, they move beyond chronically doubting and questioning the relationship they have with their partner. When this happens, they can become some of the most fun, steady and undemanding companions in the world.

SIXES AT WORK

Years ago I worked with a Six named Dan who on numerous occasions saved me from myself. At the time I was a young, overly self-assured pastor with a 37 IQ driving behind the wheel of a fast-growing church. Like any good Six, Dan kept his eye on me, and when he saw that I was about to make what he thought was a possibly calamitous decision he'd get anxious and pull me aside, saying, "Have you thought through what might happen if you take us in this direction?"

More often than not, Dan annoyed me. His need to express his doubts and ask questions about my brilliant ideas not only put the brakes on our moving forward but felt to me like he was raining on my parade. However, in some instances, if it hadn't been for his doubtfulness and questions I would have driven my parade and our fledgling church straight off an overpass.

Sixes are sharp, analytically minded troubleshooters. They love being on the underdog team trying to resurrect a company or failing program, particularly when others say it can't be done. A pitcher should be nervous when a Six comes to bat in the bottom of the ninth with the winning runner on third. They enjoy the way being the hundred-to-one shot galvanizes a team, and they're notorious for pulling a win out of their hat when the chips are down.

There are lots of things we can learn from Sixes. Most of us think and move too quickly. We make decisions on the fly precipitously, if not recklessly. But there's a clarity and wisdom that comes when we're willing to wait and think through the implications of our choices. Because they're the ultimate devil's advocate, Sixes bring that to the table wherever they work. Every business needs a loyal skeptic who isn't afraid to ask hard questions or point out the flaws in a plan. A room full of overcaffeinated, risk-tolerant entrepreneurs may not like it when a Six asks a question that pops the balloon on their big idea, but someone has to be the voice of anxiety!

Sometimes I wonder how many Sixes have bravely raised their hand and asked the one unpopular question that threw a president back on his heels long enough for him to consider what the unforeseen consequences might be were he to pursue a policy of war. We owe these clear-eyed Sixes a debt of gratitude.

Six employees will ask you *a lot* of questions, not because they're opposing you necessarily but because they're trying to figure out what they're supposed to do and to make sure someone has looked at the big picture, should something go wrong. When you're trying to launch a new initiative and you need a Six's support, listen to all their doubts or anxieties. It takes time for Sixes to think through issues and formulate questions, so publish meeting agendas in advance. Yes, all this questioning and fact checking can slow things down for the team, but if you let Sixes voice their concerns and you answer their questions, Loyalists will follow you to the ends of the earth. If not, you're flying solo.

Sixes have mixed feelings about success as well. On the eve of victory they might procrastinate because they know success will only attract attention. Sixes don't like the exposure that comes when they're in a spotlight because it leaves them vulnerable to attack. Also, Sixes don't thrive in highly competitive environments where they're pitted against their colleagues. Winning at the expense of a coworker doesn't sit well with the person who goes by the name Loyalist.

Sixes have an odd tendency to believe that thinking about something is the same as doing it. This is never more evident than in the workplace. So if you ask Sixes if they're working on that project you gave them to do, they'll say yes even if they haven't done a thing except plan and think about it! To them thinking and doing are the same thing. At work, be sure to ask follow-up questions if you really want to know where Sixes stand in terms of progress.

Because Sixes are conscientious, they tend to take on too much work, which leaves them feeling stressed out, resentful and pessimistic. When it all becomes too overwhelming they can overreact, which can ripple out and freak out other people. When this happens, get them to break tasks down into manageable steps, and encourage them to delegate more.

WINGS

Sixes with a Five wing (6w5). These Sixes are more introverted, intellectual, cautious, self-controlled and apt to seek security through allegiance to an authority figure. They gravitate toward a defined belief system and a group that shares their values. Sometimes misread as distant or aloof, 6w5s simply like to protect their privacy, engage in solitary activities and pursue hobbies. The 6w5 has a greater need for time alone, which can help them gain a broader perspective on things that contribute to their anxiety. The counter is also true, since with a Five wing the Six may ruminate too much, exacerbating unproductive thinking. Because they over-analyze things for too long without taking action, these Sixes can suffer from analysis paralysis.

Sixes with a Seven wing (6w7). Sixes with a Seven wing are a delightful surprise. Reflecting the playfulness of Seven (the Enthusiast), they are entertaining, animated and adventuresome. They are willing to risk, albeit only a little, so the boundaries of the Six are stretched to accommodate more options. But the 6w7 doesn't completely separate from their anxiety, so there is always a backup plan in case an adventure becomes a misadventure. Sixes with Seven wings are far more extroverted and willing to sacrifice themselves for loved ones than Sixes with five wings.

STRESS AND SECURITY

Stress. In stress Sixes move toward the negative side of Three, where they can become workaholics who pursue material success or hoard resources to make themselves feel more secure. In this space Sixes are more inclined to misrepresent themselves and to project an image of competency to fend off their own anxiety and give others the impression they have it all together. They won't try anything they don't think they can do successfully—which, since they already lack confidence, means they are reluctant to take necessary risks.

Security. When Sixes feel secure they move toward the positive side of Nine, where they are less prone to getting worked up about potential threats in their environment. Under the influence of the Nine's equanimity, Sixes stop planning for disasters and feel less anxious about life in general. In this space they are more light-hearted, flexible, empathic and energetic. They are accepting of others, can see life from more than one angle, and become more likely to trust their gut rather than rely on outside authority figures, groups or belief systems to interpret life for them. More trusting and less jaded, Sixes connected to the positive side of Nine can believe everything is going to be all right.

SPIRITUAL TRANSFORMATION

On the path toward spiritual growth, Sixes need to hold two conflicting things in tension: that they live in a culture that's never going to let them feel safe, and that they are safe.

> "Faith is a place of mystery, where we find the courage to believe in what we cannot see and the strength to let go of our fear of uncertainty."
>
> **BRENÉ BROWN**

How do any of us feel safe in a world where, when we turn on CNN, we see a perpetually alarmed news anchor named Wolf coming to us live from a Situation Room telling us to stay with him because in sixty seconds he will be bringing us "breaking news"? When I was a kid, breaking news meant someone had their finger on the nuclear button. Now it means Kim Kardashian has threatened to post a picture of her back bumper and "break the Internet." Our insurance ads show an unsuspecting man being T-boned at an intersection while a spokesman warns, "Trouble never takes a holiday; neither should your insurance." I don't even want to think about what will happen if I outlive my re tirement. If I'm a Four and this stuff freaks me out, I can't imagine how a Six might feel. Sixes are prone to internalize these messages of fear and imminent disaster, so it's vital for them to recognize this pattern and think twice before permitting their anxieties to take over their lives.

Sixes need to be encouraged to doubt themselves less and trust themselves more. They are stronger and more resourceful than they know. They've just been going about transformation in the wrong way. They think the antidote to fear is courage, but they can never seem to muster enough to do the job, so surely that's not the answer. What they need to develop is faith, which is different from courage in that it doesn't require certainty. Faith asks Sixes to believe and trust in something or someone bigger than they are, who will always have their back, who will never leave them but instead will be there to support them in times of crisis.

Sixes need to remember the spiritual truth that they are ultimately safe. This doesn't mean they're magically protected from disaster or calamity, just that from an eternal perspective this Story ends well. For this message to sink deep down into their bones, they will have to decide that God is either in control or he isn't, that even if everything doesn't work out as planned things will be all right.

TEN PATHS TO TRANSFORMATION FOR SIXES

1. A regular centering prayer or meditation practice is vital for every number, but particularly for Sixes. Your mind never stops working. It's filled with voices expressing vacillating opinions, doubts about other people's trustworthiness, imagined worst-case scenarios and questions about your own ability to make good decisions.

2. Be alert for unhealthy tendencies in your relationship with authority. Are you blindly following or reflexively rebelling? You'll want to find a more nuanced and conscious middle way.

3. To develop self-confidence and trust in your inner guidance system, keep a record in your journal of those times when you made and enjoyed the fruit of good decisions or survived the fallout of bad ones. Either way, you're still here!

4. Practice accepting compliments without deflecting them or being suspicious of the motivations behind the praise.

5. When playing the role of devil's advocate and pointing out the potential flaws in other people's ideas and plans, be sure to acknowledge the positive dimensions of it as well. You don't want to develop a reputation for being a wet blanket.

6. Limit your exposure to the twenty-four-hour news cycle or to books and films that unnecessarily reinforce your anxious or pessimistic view of life. (Frankly, let's all do this.)

7. Be alert in the early days of a relationship to see whether doubtful thoughts and feelings arise about your partner's commitment to you. What's causing you to alternately question or cling to them?

8. Learn to recognize the difference between legitimate fear and free-floating anxiety, and ascribe different values to them.

9. Memorize and repeat Julian of Norwich's beautiful prayer, "All shall be well, and all shall be well, and all manner of thing shall be well."

10. The contrary virtue to the deadly sin of fear isn't courage but faith, which is a gift. Pray for it.

WHAT IT'S LIKE TO BE A SEVEN

1. I'm always the first person up for a last-minute adventure.
2. I am an optimist to a fault.
3. I don't like making hard and fast commitments to things.
4. I suffer from FOMO—fear of missing out.
5. Anticipation is the best part of life.
6. People close to me say I can be argumentative and act superior.
7. Variety and spontaneity are the spice of life.
8. Sometimes I get so eager for the future I can hardly wait for it to get here.
9. It's hard for me to finish things. When I get close to the end of a project I start thinking about the next thing, and then I get so excited I sometimes just move on.
10. I usually avoid heavy conversations and confrontations.
11. When people I care about are having a hard time, I help them look at the bright side of the situation.
12. Other people think I am sure of myself, but I have lots of doubts.
13. I'm popular and have lots of friends.
14. When things get too serious for too long I usually find a way to get people to lighten up, often by telling jokes and funny stories.
15. I don't like endings, so I usually wait for people to break up with me.
16. I quickly get bored with the same routine and like to try new things.
17. Almost everything can be more fun and entertaining with a little effort.
18. I think people worry more than they should.
19. Life is better than people imagine. It's all about how you explain things to yourself.
20. I don't like it when people have expectations of me.

11

TYPE SEVEN

THE ENTHUSIAST

Just think of happy things,
and your heart will fly on wings!

PETER PAN

Healthy Sevens know that often "less is more." They are aware of the energy they have invested in manufacturing *happiness* and they know that *joy* is a gift or grace that can only be received. They have embraced a full range of human emotion and they are growing in their ability to accept life as it is rather than as they want it to be. They are able to incorporate pain and disappointment into the whole of their lives, rather than merely avoiding it. When Enthusiasts are in a healthy space, they are not only fun and adventurous but also spiritually grounded, practical and resilient.

Average Sevens reframe almost everything that is sad, limiting or could be perceived as failure, changing the narrative so that even the most negative events are recast in an affirming way. They find most of their happiness in *anticipation* and much of their sadness in the reality that their expectations are seldom realized. These Sevens entertain to feel safe and to claim their place in a group. Though they are very popular, they find commitment to be a challenge and have great trouble finishing projects, often jumping from one thing to the next.

Unhealthy Sevens see themselves and their environment as inadequate, feeling sorry for themselves and often believing they've been dealt an unfair hand. They try to avoid pain at any cost, which leads to irresponsible behavior and seeking instant gratification. These Sevens are often reckless, risking more than they can stand to lose, and are more prone to addiction than any other number.

One Saturday my wife, Anne, asked whether I would make a Whole Foods run to pick up a few items for dinner and take our eight-year-old son, Aidan, along. I'm not a cheapskate, but buying groceries at Whole Foods makes as much fiscal sense to me as buying your lawn equipment at Tiffany's. My health-nut wife's insistence that our kids eat only pesticide-free food has long been a point of contention between us. It didn't matter. Every morning for fifteen years I snuck a bag of Cheetos into their lunch bags so they could have some semblance of a normal childhood. She still can't figure out why they love me more than her. But despite my frustration, I headed to Whole Foods with Aidan.

The first thing you see when you walk into our local Whole Foods Market is the apple display—a giant, perfectly arranged pyramid of Honeycrisps and Galas. It's so imposing and artfully organized it makes you wonder whether they commissioned sculptor Andy Goldsworthy to design it. Like any young boy, the first thing Aidan did that day was charge straight toward it.

"Don't touch those apples!" I commanded in a loud voice.

Startled, Aidan jumped back from the apple display, and I turned around to continue my search for almond milk. Not five seconds later I heard a muffled thump—almost like the sound of a tennis ball landing on the roof of a canvas camping tent—followed by a few more low-toned thumps. I heard the collective gasp of my fellow customers mixed with the roar of what we now refer to in our family as the Apple-anche of 2006. When I whipped around I found Aidan on all fours, desperately grabbing at rolling fruit as if he thought he had time to collect and restack them before I discovered the nature of his evil.

Aidan looked terror stricken when he saw me walking toward him wearing my "Sinners in the Hands of an Angry God" face. But then, as if arrested by a brilliant, last-minute idea to stay his execution, he broke out in a grin, leapt to his feet . . . and began dancing.

When I say dancing, I mean "James Brown Live at the Apollo Theater in 1962" dancing. Now brought up short, I watched as he segued into the famous John Travolta peace-sign-across-the-eyes dance from the movie *Pulp Fiction*. Where does an eight-year-old learn such things? Few things will dissolve a father's fury quite like the sight of a giggling little boy wearing a "Life is Good" T-shirt dancing in a scree of apples. Lord knows I tried, but I couldn't prevent myself from laughing along with everyone else in the aisle as he thrust out his little butt and moved into doing the twist. How do you reprimand a kid like that? For the umpteenth time in his brief life Aidan had managed to turn a crime into a comedy.

Now a freshman in college, Aidan moonwalks whenever we pass the apple display at Whole Foods as a reminder to me of how he managed to elude certain death that day. And yes, it still makes me laugh. He's a quintessential Seven on the Enneagram.

THE SEVEN'S DEADLY SIN

I want to be a Seven. When healthy, they might be my favorite number on the Enneagram.

Sevens embody joy and a boundless love for life. Most mornings they burst into life like kids who just found out it's a snow day. At the same time, I'm not naive. Because Aidan and many of my closest friends are Sevens on the Enneagram, I'm well acquainted with their dark side. As is the case with every Enneagram type, what's best about their personality is what's worst about their personality. Their gift is also their curse.

Scratch the vibrant paint on the surface of a Seven and what you'll find underneath is the need to avoid pain. I can't say that strongly enough—Sevens don't want to feel unpleasant emotions, particularly that swirl of fear and emptiness they register at their core. No one enjoys feeling frightened, sad, bored, angry, disappointed or frustrated, but for Sevens, emotions like these are intolerable.

I thought for sure I was a Seven when I learned that *gluttony* is their deadly sin. Spend a week in Italy with me and you'll know why I mistyped myself. But for Sevens, the sin of gluttony isn't about their fondness for *pennete al salmone* as much as a reflection of their compulsive need to devour positive experiences, stimulating ideas and fine material things in order to fend off suffering, hurtful memories and a feeling of chronic deprivation.

FAMOUS SEVENS
Robin Williams
Wolfgang Amadeus Mozart
Stephen Colbert

Sevens crave stimulation. Ask one how much is enough and they'll say, "Just a little more." And that's the problem—there's never enough, at least not to satisfy a Seven's voracious appetite. The psychiatrist and author Gabor Maté likens addicts to "hungry ghosts," ravished creatures who have "scrawny necks, small mouths, emaciated limbs and large, bloated, empty bellies." It's a ghoulish visual, but it's an apt description of the

Seven's dilemma. Like "hungry ghosts," Sevens cope with their inner tumult by gorging themselves on interesting ideas, acquiring choice material possessions, jamming their calendars with activities and adventures, fantasizing about a future filled with exciting possibilities, and planning their next great escapade.

According to the Enneagram, the opposite of gluttony is sobriety. For Sevens, sobriety doesn't mean giving up drinking but rather slowing down, living in the present moment, exercising self-restraint, reining in their restless "monkey minds" and getting down to the business of ordinary life. You know, all the stuff regular civilians like us have to do.

All of us have ways of defending ourselves against pain. For Sevens, it's keeping things lively and positive. The question Sevens are always asking themselves is, *How can I jam as many pleasurable experiences into this moment as possible?* Their source of satisfaction is never found within them or in the present moment; it's always external and in the far-distant future. There's always something they haven't tried, something more to do, some new exploit to plan. All this hopped-up behavior is how Sevens divert their attention away from the unacknowledged and unintegrated losses and anxieties that haunt them. Most people know that unpleasant feelings and truths can't be avoided indefinitely, but not Sevens. They believe they can outrun them forever. As Richard Rohr says, "Sevens try to imagine a life where there is no Good Friday, and it's Easter all the time."

It's hard to get your head around it, but Sevens are every bit as fearful as Fives and Sixes. Where they differ is in the way they defend themselves against it—Fives ward off fear with knowledge, Sixes with pessimism and Sevens with inexhaustible optimism.

If you gave me only three minutes to describe the coping strategy of a Seven I'd simply sing you a few verses of the song "I Whistle a Happy Tune" from the musical *The King and I*:

Whenever I feel afraid
I hold my head erect
And whistle a happy tune
So no one will suspect I'm afraid.

So it is with Sevens, whose determination to deny entrance to negative feelings winds up costing them their most authentic self. They fool themselves as well—and no amount of novel experiences and exciting adventures can ever quite fill that void.

ALL ABOUT SEVENS OR ENTHUSIASTS

Living for tomorrow and turning a blind eye to the inevitable dolorous ordeals of today may sound like a great way to go through life, and there are certainly times when Sevens' indomitable optimism is a gift. But sometimes such behavior can create problems for Sevens and those who love them.

> "Let us step into the night and pursue that flighty temptress, adventure."
> *J. K. ROWLING*

Sevens want to avoid pain. Sevens believe they can *think* their way out of pain. I once asked my friend Juliette to describe what life is like for her as a Seven. Among other things, she shared how she copes with negative emotions by intellectualizing them. "For me worry or stress are easier to deal with because I can work with them in my mind," she said. "Feelings like disappointment, grief or sadness are much harder because I actually have to feel them."

When I asked Juliette whether she'd ever seen a therapist, she laughed and said, "Yes, but whenever a counselor succeeds at getting me too close to a painful topic I instantly tell a joke or a funny story about something goofy the kids did that week to get them off topic and around negative emotions." Sevens will go out of their way to avoid pain and introspection, which makes the self-awareness that's needed for growth more of a challenge for Sevens than for most other types.

But the ways that they avoid pain are just so freaking entertaining. If my experience in Whole Foods with Aidan tells you anything, it's that charm is one of the first lines of defense for Sevens. Angry parents, teachers and coaches find it all but impossible to discipline puckish Sevens. They can talk their way out of almost anything. If Adam and Eve had been Sevens we'd all still be living in the Garden of Eden.

When situations become too emotionally intense or distressing, Sevens will feel an irrepressible urge to lighten things up a little. They're the ones who slip a grimace-worthy joke into a eulogy, laugh uncontrollably during a sad scene in a movie or feign a bad case of the hiccups to distract people while their boss is announcing mandatory layoffs. While the choices Sevens make to deal with anxiety or unpalatable feelings can earn them popularity for being the class clown, they can't seem to make a connection between their immature behaviors and the fact that people say they lack intellectual and emotional depth. If they never do their work, adult Sevens develop a reputation for not being able to swim outside the shallow end of the pool.

The last thing I would want is a world without Sevens. They're wonderful human beings, particularly when they've learned to face up to the fact that life consists of both agony and ecstasy moments. The problem is too many settle for being Peter Pan—they never want to grow up.

Sevens are vulnerable to addiction. Several mornings a week I attend twelve-step meetings. It's not often I see so many Sevens gathered in one place at one time. Not all Sevens become addicts, but their impulsivity and difficulty with delaying gratification, combined with their desire to escape afflictive emotions at all costs, make them more addiction-prone than any other number on the Enneagram. Why suffer a flood of awful and frightening emotions when half a bottle of wine, a few hours on a porn site, a handful of oxycontin, a blackjack game, a quart of ice cream or a shopping binge offers an easy, fast-acting source of pain relief?

"I'm not an alcoholic, but one day I realized that whenever I go to parties I end up drinking three glasses of wine to put a protective layer between myself and that one Eeyore-like person who wants to drag me into a conversation about a depressing topic," Juliette told me. "I pretty much don't like anything or anyone who brings me down."

In my opinion Sevens are particularly vulnerable to pornography addictions. Think about it—you get to enjoy an erotic rush that numbs negative feelings, and as an added bonus you can trick yourself into believing you're having an intimate experience with another person without having to step up to the plate and make a commitment to them—something Sevens are hesitant to do. Gambling, too, is a particular temptation for Sevens, whose natural optimism convinces them that this next hand will be a winner or that their luck is about to turn. Gambling is all about the things that Sevens find attractive, like exciting possibilities and future good fortune, so it's all too easy for them to be pulled in. Like I said, not all Sevens become addicts, but they have to watch themselves.

Sevens are spin doctors. Sevens are masters at what's termed "reframing." In the blink of an eye they can take a bad situation and recast it in a positive light to skirt feeling the pain you and I would experience if the same thing happened to us. This defense mechanism is unconscious, instantaneous and impressive.

At one time my friend Bob was one of the most sought-after music video producers in the world. After a while he became so bored and disgusted with directing four-minute movies of half-naked women dancing to atrocious music that he promised himself he'd never produce one again.

Recently over lunch Bob told me how a few months earlier he had reneged on his vow by agreeing to shoot a video for a big country act because "the money was just too good to pass up." That morning the artist's manager had called to tell him they were disappointed with his footage and were hiring another director to reshoot the video.

"Honestly, I think it's a blessing," Bob explained. "I see it as God's confirmation that I should stay away from making music videos and continue down my new career path."

Bob and I have been friends a long time and he's pretty well versed in the Enneagram, so I asked him whether his response to the call wasn't just a textbook example of a Seven duct taping a silver lining to a black cloud. He danced around my question until he finally gave up and laughed, saying, "I always have a pocket full of silver linings."

"You ought to get around to having your feelings about losing that gig," I said.

"I'll *think* about it," he said, knowing that was the perfect answer from someone in the Head Triad.

(For the record, Bob's new career path involves hanging out the door of a helicopter and shooting aerial videos of lions running around the Serengeti. He sells the films to adventure tour companies who use them as promotional pieces for their websites. I know, it's perfect beyond words.)

Watch and be amazed when Sevens start to rationalize. If you call Sevens on the carpet for acting selfishly or having a bad attitude, or you caution them against making a dumb decision, they'll climb the barricade and defend to the death the reasonableness of their position. They'll come up with a million good reasons for doing whatever it is they want to do no matter what it will cost them or others. Their litany of justifications is no more than a strategy against having to feel guilty for being selfish or stupid for making an unwise decision.

Because they're bright and such quick learners, Sevens can develop an inflated sense of their own giftedness, intelligence and achievement, and become arrogant. They love to debate ideas and are so articulate and fast on their feet that they rarely lose in a battle of wits even when they know less about the topic than their opponent. They can definitely suffer from a superiority complex.

Sevens are escapologists on par with David Blaine. They always need and will have an escape hatch or backup plan in the event life gets scary, boring or uncomfortable. On our way into a movie theater one night, my friend Bob and I passed an art gallery where people were gathering for the opening of a photography exhibit. "Perfect!" he said. "If the movie stinks we can slip out and head over to that instead." It's stunning, really.

Sevens don't want to be tied down. Sevens need flexibility and avoid making long-term, option-limiting commitments. Anne and I often say we regret not knowing the Enneagram when our kids were growing up. In fifth grade Aidan showed promise as a drummer, but he bristled whenever we suggested he join the school band. Having to make a commitment to attending band practice twice a week after school sounded more like voluntary incarceration than fun. Anne and I eventually convinced Aidan to try band just once. His response afterward was predictable. "I hated it," he groaned. "The band director said I had to stick to playing the notes on the page like everyone else. I like to *improvise!*"

> "It's never too late to have a happy childhood."
>
> **TOM ROBBINS**

From personal experience, I can tell you not wanting to stick to playing what's on the page is a pattern with many Sevens. Helen Palmer calls them the Epicures because of the way they delight in all the best possibilities in life. If you don't believe me, take a Seven to dinner. They're usually the first person to smell what the menu special is. "Holy smokes, do you smell that curry?" they'll revel, with a euphoric expression on their face.

If you really want to see Sevens swoon, take them to a buffet-style restaurant. They're the guys in the line who load their plate because they can't bear the idea of not sampling a little bit of everything! If you take them to a restaurant they've been to before, they definitely won't order the same thing a second time, even if they loved it. What kind of person would settle for the same old fare when they can try something different and exciting?

Sevens live for the next adventure. Sevens know exactly what Andy Warhol meant when he said, "The idea of waiting for something makes it more exciting." These pleasure-seekers savor anticipation. For them, the best part of a meal, a party or a trip isn't when it comes; it's the thrill of expectancy leading up to it. This is why Sevens sometimes feel a little let down when the prime rib appears, the party guests arrive, or they're actually standing at the base of the Eiffel Tower. The real deal couldn't possibly live up to their expectations. The pleasure is in the waiting, not the sating. (Yes, I came up with that last line. Feel free to use it.)

Sevens make sure they always have something to do lest an adverse feeling break through a crack in their schedule. "I know I'm anxious when I keep looking at the calendar to see what's coming up," my friend Juliette confessed to me.

Aidan spent his junior year of high school studying classics in Italy. A few weeks before it was time to return home he called to tell us about a summer program in classics being offered at Oxford. "It would look great on my college applications," he said. "Not only that, but the flights from Italy to England are cheap right now." I knew exactly what my champion rationalizer was doing. Rather than feel sad about having to say goodbye to friends and face the prospect of coming home to attend his tenth and final year of summer camp, he had jumped on his computer to trawl around the Internet in search of another adventure.

Unfortunately, Sevens have so much trouble remaining in the present moment they never fully enjoy the adventures they're having because they're already thinking and planning the next one.

SEVENS AS CHILDREN

Sevens often describe childhoods filled with tree swings, lazy summer afternoons spent fishing with Uncle Henry, winter days building snow forts and going to sleep-away camp. Seriously? No one gets off this easy.

If you succeed at getting Sevens to open up about their childhood, they will describe times when they were made to feel overwhelmed or abandoned and without support—the night Mom and Dad sat them down to announce they were splitting up, their brother contracting a lifelong serious illness that sucked Mom's attention away from them for years, the last-minute move that happened so quickly they barely had time to say goodbye to their friends, or the loss of someone whose death felt more like a desertion.

In their developmental years, Sevens heard the wounding message, "You're on your own. No one's here to support or take care of you." In response Sevens said, "I'll do it if no one else will." But whereas Fives dealt with this same crisis by reducing their need to depend on anyone and Sixes solved it by attempting to anticipate every possible disaster, young Sevens' strategy involved creating a pain-free Neverland in their mind where they could hide out and think happy thoughts until their pain dissolved.

Regardless of the underlying factors, as kids Sevens adopt a strategy of going up into their heads to plan adventures, entertain captivating ideas and imagine a life where the sky's the limit to diffuse scary emotions they fear will overwhelm them. These kids are not merely entertained by Peter Pan; they are the ones who, like Peter, truly believe in magic. They live in imaginary scenes in their rooms, their backyards and the back seat of the car. They are happy to play with others and content when they are alone.

Curiosity defines Sevens, which is part of the gift they are to themselves and to the world. But boundless curiosity is also part of the problem. Rules are necessary, but Seven kids find them insufferably limiting. The grass is always greener just beyond the fence line. When they are restrained by limits of some kind, they retreat into their heads, where they rely on their imagination to provide all the entertainment they need until the restrictions are lifted.

Seven children are not achievement-oriented so much as experience-oriented. They like the fun part of Boy Scouts but aren't terribly interested in earning badges or advancing toward a goal. That's not to say they're lazy—far from it. Sevens are always on the go: they're the kids who want to stay longer and play longer. Limitless energy is available day after day in their world, and they never seem to want to stop.

Emotionally, young Sevens are already learning the art of denying negative feelings. For these children, feeling good instead of bad seems to be a choice, so they are confused by sadness in others. They move away from the negative and toward whatever is positive, even if that means reframing their experiences to make for a happier narrative. Sevens learn to move away from fear and pain early in childhood, and they carry that strategy into adulthood.

SEVENS IN RELATIONSHIPS

There's never a dull moment with Sevens. More than any other type, they need spontaneity. They are either planning and talking about their next escapade or asking you to join them on one. Whether it's a night of exotic fare at a new ethnic restaurant, a day of naked skydiving, a lecture on cubist art at the museum, an evening of opera or a last-minute road trip, Sevens are the first to yell "Shotgun!" and race you to the car. If you're not ready and raring to go somewhere at a moment's notice, your relationship with a Seven probably won't last.

Sevens want nothing to do with confining relationships. They're classic commitment phobes. To Sevens, "stuck" and "commitment" look and feel like the same thing. As Helen Palmer observes, because they treasure their independence Sevens have to be made to believe a relational commitment is their idea rather than something you imposed on them. Over the long term, some of them have a hard time sticking to a partner through thick and thin.

If you are or have ever been in a committed relationship with a Seven, you know what wonderful companions they are. Because their talk style is *storytelling*, they can keep a group on the edge of their seats while they excitedly act out a story of something that happened to them. They're always interested in your inner life. They'll want to know your life story and draw you into their exciting world. At times, however, the Seven's fascination with your life is more a symptom of their gluttony than a sign of genuine interest. Regardless, your relationship with a Seven will have to keep evolving over time or they'll start looking for the fire exit.

Fear of the bad feelings that arise in conflict will trigger denial in a Seven. You might have to light your hair on fire before you get a Seven to face up to the fact that something's not working. Of course, the pivotal moment comes when Sevens can't stall having to decide about whether to make a long-term commitment to you or not.

For some Sevens, the end of a relationship can be very difficult. It's hard to outrun or repress the sadness associated with a breakup. But some Sevens and their friends have told me that they can walk away from relationships with hardly any negative feelings at all. This repression of emotions can make some Sevens appear callous or lacking in empathy.

Sevens always want to keep their options open. They're the people who when you ask them to join you for dinner on Friday night will say they'll get back to you. After all, what if someone asks them to do something more exciting between now and Friday?

It's not unusual to hear a Seven's friends say they have felt abandoned by them on more than one occasion. They tend to overcommit socially, since a Seven abhors a vacuum and an empty calendar threatens them with boredom. Sometimes, their well-established relationships get last priority when Sevens rush off chasing new friends and exhilarating experiences.

People unknowingly rely on Sevens to bring their supply of infectious enthusiasm to every activity they do with them. We figured this out on a recent family trip to Italy. Every morning our family would meet over breakfast to plan the day's activities. One day in Florence, Aidan said he wanted to take a gondola ride on the Arno River, while the rest of us voted to make the famous climb to the top of the duomo, the city's main cathedral. Like all Sevens, Aidan will occasionally become ornery when others put the kibosh on his plans, but on this day he shrugged and agreed to go.

There are 463 very steep stairs to the top of the duomo. If Aidan had been his usual exuberant self, the ascent would have been a breeze. All the way up he would have been telling jokes or racing ahead and yelling back to us to hurry up. That day, however, Aidan was more oatmeal than ice cream. He wasn't acting sullen or exacting revenge on us. What we'd chosen to do had simply turned the dial settings that control the flame on his enthusiasm from its default setting of high down to medium low. Climbing the duomo without the benefit of Aidan's characteristic enthusiasm felt like climbing Everest without the benefit of oxygen.

My kids are well-versed in the Enneagram, so over dinner that night we talked about how much we as a family had come to depend on Aidan to infuse our activities with his ebullient spirit. We assured him he didn't need to play the role of the court jester for us anymore. But we had learned our lesson—if the next morning he had announced he wanted to straighten the Tower of Pisa we'd have agreed to help so long as he was pumped about it. We know now that there ain't no sunshine when he's gone.

Sevens would rather eat glass than suffer boredom. When it surfaces Sevens get hyperactive and overly talkative, their minds race faster than usual, and they become bad-tempered. I'm often reminded of a friend who has two young boys who go off the deep end when they have nothing to do and begin racing circles around the house like Adderall-crazed racehorses. To interrupt the circuit he has to grab them, make them take ten deep breaths and repeat the phrase "Be here now." Similarly, when adult Sevens begin frantically running around or flitting from one project to the next without finishing any, they need friends or partners to stop them and say "get present."

Sevens are fascinated with other people's lives, and they're counter-intuitively attracted to people who have suffered. It's as if they instinctively know these folks possess an emotional depth they yearn for but don't know how to develop. It also may be they don't want to face the fact that suffering is the only point of entry into a deeper life.

To be clear, Sevens can enter dark emotional spaces, but they can only stay there for so long before they have to escape. Many Sevens balk when you describe their need to avoid pain. "I'm always listening to melancholy movie soundtracks, spending time alone and thinking about my life," they protest. It's true; from time to time Sevens will choose to dip their feet in the waters of sadness, but it's always on their own terms and under their control.

SEVENS AT WORK

Sevens would kill for the opportunity to take over Anthony Bourdain's job as host of the cable food and travel show *Parts Unknown*. To jet the globe exploring new cultures, meeting fascinating people, eating strange meals, and never knowing what lies around the next corner— are you kidding? Gigs like that don't come along very often, but Sevens need to find work in similarly fast-paced, creative environments that afford them independence, a variety of activities and flexibility.

Sevens are dreamers and initiators. Give them a dry-erase marker and a white board and step out of the way. Their ability to synthesize information from a wide range of subject areas, spot unseen patterns and connect the dots inside complex bodies of knowledge, and notice where systems overlap make them prolific idea generators. Add to that Sevens' keen analytical skills and their capacity to envision an organization's preferred future, and you've got someone who will adrenalize teams and make an invaluable contribution to advancing the mission of any corporation.

Sevens are rock stars when it comes to working on short-term projects or getting start-up companies off the ground. Their optimism and creative juice and sprite energy move things along at a quick pace. Be forewarned, however: Sevens aren't managers or maintainers, so you'll need to find someone else to oversee the execution phase while you set the Seven loose on a new venture. Also, Sevens are marvelous team players. Friendly and popular, they bring variety and some much-needed spontaneity to the workplace.

Sevens don't like being told what to do, so working for a controlling leader who imposes too many limits on them rarely works out well. Sometimes they manipulate authority figures with charm and charisma, but this is not a tenable situation for the long term. Sevens work best under conditions that offer both firmness and flexibility. Yes, they need to be held accountable to keeping on track, but it's best to give talented Sevens a long leash, a multifaceted job description and encouragement to stay the course. Sevens can make great leaders as long as they don't have to carry the weight of too much responsibility. Sevens often have trouble with professional decision making. After all, saying yes to one thing means saying no to another, and that means reducing options.

WINGS

Sevens with a Six wing (7w6). These sevens are more settled than other Sevens. Fueled by the conscientiousness of the Six, they give both projects and people more time before moving on to the next thing. These Sevens are sensitive and a bit more anxious, but they successfully use charm to disarm. Once they commit to a relationship they have a good chance of staying connected and working out challenges in it. These Sevens are dutiful and loyal to family and friends. They are funny, entertaining and accepting of others.

Sevens with an Eight wing (7w8). The 7w8s are competitive, bold and aggressive. Reflecting the Eight's characteristic bravado, they are persuasive and assertive in relation to their ideas and agendas, and they usually get their way. Still, they are playful, and having a good time is more important to them than gaining power. These Sevens are easily bored, so they often start things they don't finish. They enjoy being in relationships as long as they can contribute to the happiness of their partner. Living inside an unhappy relationship is very frustrating for these Sevens, and yet endings are devastating.

STRESS AND SECURITY

Stress. When they're under stress, Sevens can adopt the unhealthy and perfectionistic behaviors of Ones. They become pessimistic, judgmental and argumentative. They start blaming others for their problems and lapse into black-and-white thinking.

Security. When Sevens feel secure they can start to behave like healthy Fives. Here they stop consuming and start contributing, are more comfortable with silence and solitude, become more serious, and begin to think about the meaning and purpose of their lives. Sevens on the positive side of One explore things on a much deeper level than other Sevens and are able to name and face their fears. Sevens connected to the positive side of Five can experience satisfaction in the truest sense of the word.

SPIRITUAL TRANSFORMATION

What would we do without Sevens? They bring so much joie de vivre to our lives! Who else can awaken our childlike wonder, rescue us from taking ourselves too seriously or help us appreciate the miracle of life quite like Sevens can?

But here's a hard truth: pain is unavoidable. On the road to spiritual transformation, Sevens have to learn how to embrace and steward their suffering rather than run from it.

As Michel de Montaigne once said, "He who fears he shall suffer already suffers what he fears." In other words, Sevens' strategies for avoiding pain create more suffering for them. Until they learn this Sevens are like addicts who will have to keep upping the dosage of fascinating ideas, novel experiences and self-generated pleasant feelings to repress the ones they want to keep outside their conscious awareness. It's time for Sevens to stop consuming and start contributing. True happiness and satisfaction can't be taken by force or manufactured whenever we need them; they are the result of living a focused and productive life that gives something back to the world. As Thomas Merton wrote, "In a world of tension and breakdown it is necessary for there to be those who seek to integrate their inner lives not by avoiding anguish and running away from problems, but by facing them in their naked reality and in their ordinariness."

The healing message Sevens need to hear and believe is *God will take care of you.* I know, easier said than done. It will take courage, determination, honesty, the help of a counselor or a spiritual director, and understanding friends to help Sevens confront painful memories and to encourage them to stay with afflictive feelings as they arise in the present moment. If Sevens cooperate with the process, they'll grow a deep heart and become a truly integrated person.

TEN PATHS TO TRANSFORMATION FOR SEVENS

1. Practice restraint and moderation. Get off the treadmill that tells you more is always better.

2. You suffer from "monkey mind." Develop a daily practice of meditation to free yourself from your tendency to jump from one idea, topic or project to the next.

3. Develop and practice the spiritual discipline of solitude on a regular basis.

4. Unflinchingly reflect on the past and make a list of the people who have hurt you or whom you have hurt; then forgive them and yourself. Make amends where necessary.

5. Give yourself a pat on the back whenever you allow yourself to feel negative emotions like anxiety, sadness, frustration, envy or disappointment without letting yourself run away to escape them. It's a sign you're starting to grow up!

6. Bring yourself back to the present moment whenever you begin fantasizing about the future or making too many plans for it.

7. Exercise daily to burn off excess energy.

8. You don't like being told you have potential because it means you'll feel pressure to buckle down and commit to cultivating a specific talent, which will inevitably limit your options. But you do have potential, so what career or life path would you like to commit yourself to for the long haul? Take concrete steps to make good on the gifts God has given you.

9. Get a journal and record your answers to questions like "What does my life mean? What memories or feelings am I running from? Where's the depth I yearn to have that will complement my intelligence?" Don't abandon this exercise until it's finished.

10. Make a commitment that when a friend or partner is hurting, you will try to simply be present for them while they are in pain without trying to artificially cheer them up.

12

SO NOW WHAT?

THE BEGINNING OF LOVE

The beginning of love is the will to let those we love
be perfectly themselves, the resolution not to twist them to fit
our own image. If in loving them we do not love what they are,
but only their potential likeness to ourselves, then we
do not love them: we only love the reflection
of ourselves we find in them.

THOMAS MERTON

Suzanne's friend Rebecca is a nurse who works with children with profound visual impairment. As part of her job, she leads support groups for parents whose kids have just received a diagnosis. These parents, mostly young mothers, are confused, hurt and sometimes angry, and Rebecca provides guidance about navigating challenges they never suspected life would visit on them.

Apart from the practical advice, the most invaluable part of the workshops comes when Rebecca hands the parents eyeglasses that correlate to each child's specific disability. Almost always, the parents burst into tears. "I had no idea that this is the way my child sees the world," they tell her. Once they have the experience of observing through their children's eyes, they never experience the world in quite the same way again. They may still be angry about the diagnosis, but they're not frustrated with their child, because even a brief exposure to the reality of how hard life is for these kids inspires in their parents only compassion.

This is the gift of the Enneagram. Sometimes people talk about the Enneagram as a tool that reveals the lens through which people see the world. When you realize that your Loyalist Six husband views it as a place filled with danger and uncertainty, and he in turn understands that when you get up in the morning you as a Performer Three feel an urgent need to compete and excel at everything you do, it's amazing how much more compassion you can have for each other. Everything isn't so personal anymore. You understand that your loved one's behavior is born out of a singular biography, a particular wound, a fractured vision of life.

Now that you understand the basics of the Enneagram, Suzanne and I hope two things happen for you. The first is simply that it sparks greater compassion for others and for yourself.

> "Compassion is a verb."
> **THICH NHAT HANH**

If we all could have nine pairs of Enneagram glasses and swap them, we could be moved to extend infinitely more grace and understanding to one another. Such compassion is the foundation of relationships. It changes everything.

The Enneagram shows us that we can't change the way other people see, but we can try to experience the world through their eyes and help them change what they *do* with what they see. I like the way Buddhist teacher Thich Nhat Hanh explains this. "When our hearts are small, our understanding and compassion are limited, and we suffer. We can't accept or tolerate others and their shortcomings, and we demand that they change," he says. "But when our hearts expand, these same things don't make us suffer anymore. We have a lot of understanding and compassion and can embrace others. We accept others as they are, and then they have a chance to transform."

Ponder that last line for a moment. It's when we stop trying to change people and simply love them that they actually have a shot at transformation. The Enneagram is a tool that awakens our compassion for people just as they are, not the people we wish they would become so our lives would become easier.

After reading this book, we hope you feel stirred to widen the circle of compassion to include more and more people around you—even yourself. I said earlier in the book that I long for people to know that God beholds us with the same soft gaze the adoring mother beholds her sleeping infant with. If we could look at ourselves with that same quality of affection, how much healing could take place in our souls?

This idea of self-compassion raises the other issue we want you to take away from this book: every number on the Enneagram teaches us something about the nature and character of the God who made us. Inside each number is a hidden gift that reveals something about God's heart. So when you are tempted to prosecute yourself for the flaws in your own character, remember that each type is at its core a signpost pointing us to travel toward and embrace an aspect of God's character that we need.

Ones show us God's perfection and his desire to restore the world to its original goodness, while Twos witness to God's unstoppable, selfless giving. Threes remind us about God's glory, and Fours about the creativity and pathos of God. Fives show God's omniscience, Sixes God's steadfast love and loyalty, and Sevens God's childlike joy and delight in creation. Eights mirror God's power and intensity, while Nines reflect God's love of peace and desire for union with his children.

The problems arise when we exaggerate these characteristics, when we grab hold of a single trait and turn it into an ultimate value or an idol. When we privilege one of these nine characteristics above all else, that's when it becomes grotesque and unrecognizable or—dare I say—sinful.

Ones' passion to improve the world goes bad when they start to believe that in order to be loved they have to be perfect and not make mistakes. Twos' self-donating love devolves into an unhealthy codependence. Threes take their love of glory and disfigure it into a narcissistic need for constant praise. Fours descend into self-absorption as they give free rein to their overcharged feelings, while Fives have nearly the opposite problem, withdrawing into their minds and cutting themselves off from the unavoidable risks intrinsic to all human relationships. Sixes are unable to trust in a future in which God is already waiting for them, and Sevens flee the pain that deepens the soul in favor of a party that only distracts it. Eights' need to be right and to challenge others can deteriorate into intimidating the weak, and Nines' desire to avoid conflict at all costs means that they are all too willing to accept peace at any price.

> "For me to be a saint means to be myself."
>
> **THOMAS MERTON**

Behind each of these distortions is a misguided strategy to grab for happiness and love the way Adam and Eve overreached and grabbed for fruit. We are trying to steal that which can only be received as a gift from God.

Part of the Enneagram's goal is to help us relax our paralytic grip on that one dimension of God's character so we can open our hands to receive the other characteristics of God our clenched fists will not allow. A One may never fully stop reaching for perfection, but he can open his hands to receive the gifts other numbers hold. A Six is not going to entirely stop being anxious, but she can begin to perceive and cultivate the gifts that come with a Seven's joie de vivre or an Eight's assertiveness, counterbalancing her own anxiety.

What we all want to do is seek health within our own number and respect and recognize that we have access to all the gifts of these other numbers. What we're after is *integritas*, or wholeness.

In his landmark work *New Seeds of Contemplation* the Catholic monk Thomas Merton wrote, "For me to be a saint means to be myself. Therefore the problem of sanctity and salvation is in fact the problem of finding out who I am and of discovering my true self."

Though it has taken me twenty years to grasp the meaning of Merton's insight, I understand it now. We most delight and reflect the glory of God when we discover and reclaim our God-given identity, with which we lost connection shortly after our arrival in this fallen world.

We owe it to the God who created us, to ourselves, to the people we love and to all with whom we share this troubled planet to become "saints." How else can we run and complete the errand on which God sent us here?

And now allow us the joy of passing on to you John O'Donohue's Blessing for Solitude, which Br. Dave prayed over me as I embarked on my Enneagram journey of self-discovery and self-knowledge.

> May you recognize in your life the presence, power, and light of your soul.
>
> May you realize that you are never alone, that your soul in its brightness and belonging connects you intimately with the rhythm of the universe.
>
> May you have respect for your individuality and difference.
>
> May you realize that the shape of your soul is unique, that you have a special destiny here, that behind the façade of your life there is something beautiful and eternal happening.
>
> May you learn to see your self with the same delight, pride, and expectation with which God sees you in every moment.

Amen. Let it be so.

ACKNOWLEDGMENTS

Ian Morgan Cron

My grateful appreciation to my literary agent, Kathy Helmers, my editors, Jana Riess and Allison Rieck, for courage under fire, Jim and Solveig Chaffee and Chaffee Management, Mike and Gail Hyatt for friendship and hospitality, Karen and Steve Anderson for their love and the beautiful Cottage on Main in Franklin, Tennessee, Joe Stabile, Michael and Julianne Cusick, Bishop Ian Douglas, Don Chaffer, Anthony Skinner, Chris and Laurel Scarlata, Melissa Greene, Chuck Royce, Rob Mathes, Shauna and Aaron Niequist, Laura Addis, Josh Graves, Hunter Mobley, Steve and Debbie Taylor, Jenny and Sam Owen, Paul and Lisa Michalski, Jim Lemler and my Christ Church Greenwich family, Jeff Crosby, Cindy Bunch and all the good folks at IVP, and all who shared their stories with me that I might share them with you.

Suzanne Stabile

Most of all I want to thank my husband, Joe Stabile. His unending commitment to me and to our marriage is both honoring and challenging as he insists that we commit our lives to building the kingdom. Our children, son-in-laws and grandchildren are my motivation for wanting to do my part to make the world a better place, and I am so grateful for each of them. Thank you Joey and Billy, Will, Sam; Jenny and Cory, Noah, Elle, Piper; Joel, Joley; and B. J. and Devon for oh so much!

Father Richard Rohr invited me into the study of this ancient wisdom, so whatever my teaching has become is easily traced back to him. There are no words to adequately thank the thousands of people who have shared their weekends and their stories with me over the past twenty-five years. They are the reason the information I gathered about the Enneagram became wisdom.

I would have never imagined myself coauthoring a book like this, but Ian Cron did, and I am grateful. His respect for my work with the Enneagram and his way of making room for me in this project has given me a new energy for the challenges that are yet to come. Thanks to Sheryl Fullerton for being my literary agent and, of far greater importance, for being my friend. I'm grateful for Kathy Helmers for representing us to IVP. Special thanks to our editor, Cindy Bunch, and to Jeff Crosby and Andrew Bronson and all at IVP who helped us find our way as coauthors and who helped me find a place to stand as a novice in the world of publishing.

There are so many people who give their time and energy to the work of Life in the Trinity Ministry. Carolyn Teel, my best friend for forty-six years; Mike George, Joe's best friend for fifty-two years, and his wife Patsy; Ann Leick, The Community of Life in the Trinity Ministry, Cindy Short, B. C. and Karen Hosch, Dr. John and Stephanie Burk, Tanya Dohoney, John Brimm, Tom Hoekstra, Jane Henry and Luci Neuman, who dreamed of a future for LTM that we could hardly imagine. Dr. Shirley Corbitt and Marge Buchanan, thank you for supporting me for literally all of my adult life. Meredith Inman, Laura Addis and Jim Chaffee for all the work you do on my behalf; and Dr. Bob Hughes, thank you for insisting that I believe I am wanted.

I am, and have been, well loved by many people who encourage me to live my life well and to do what is mine to do in regard to teaching the Enneagram. To each of you, I am so very thankful.

And finally to P. F. Chang's. When Ian called and suggested we write this book I took a few days for some discernment and prayer before giving him an answer. During that time Joe and I ate dinner at the Chang's in Dallas. My fortune cookie contained this message: *"You are a lover of books. You should write a book some day."*

Respectfully and with gratitude we want to acknowledge and express our thanks to these great teachers who have led the way for us and for so many others in the study of the Enneagram. We owe them a great debt of gratitude for the ways in which their insights have helped our work.

Richard Rohr, OFM
Claudio Naranjo
Renee Baron
Andreas Ebert
Don Riso
Russ Hudson
Helen Palmer
David Daniels
Virginia Price
Beatrice Chestnut
Kathleen Hurley
Theodore Donson
Elizabeth Wagele
Thomas Condon
Susan Reynolds
Sandra Maitri
Lynette Sheppard
Suzanne Zuercher, OSB
Clarence Thomson
Margaret Keyes
Roxanne Howe-Murphy

NOTES

1 A CURIOUS THEORY OF UNKNOWN ORIGIN

18   *May you recognize:* John O'Donohue, "For Solitude," in *To Bless the Space Between Us: A Book of Blessings* (New York: Doubleday, 2008).

2 FINDING YOUR TYPE

23   *"The original, shimmering self":* Frederick Buechner, *Telling Secrets* (San Francisco: HarperSanFrancisco, 2000).

24   *"Before we can become who we really are":* Thomas Merton, *No Man Is an Island* (Boston: Mariner Books, 2000).

24   *"pure diamond, blazing with the invisible light":* Thomas Merton, *Conjectures of a Guilty Bystander* (New York: Doubleday Religion, 2009).

30   *"Sins are fixations":* Richard Rohr and Andreas Ebert, *The Enneagram: A Christian Perspective* (New York: Crossroad, 2001).

31   *"No one should work with the Enneagram":* David G. Benner, *The Gift of Being Yourself: The Sacred Call to Self-Discovery* (Downers Grove, IL: InterVarsity Press, 2004).

34   *"there is one quality that trumps all":* Anthony K. Tjan, "How Leaders Become Self-Aware," *Harvard Business Review*, July 19, 2012, https://hbr.org/2012/07/how-leaders-become-self-aware&cm_sp=Article-_-Links-_-End%20of%20Page%20Recirculation.

35   *Motorola, the Oakland A's:* Jean Seligman and Nadine Joseph, "To Find Self, Take a Number," *Newsweek,* September 11, 1994, www.newsweek.com/find-self-take-number-188156.

37   *"the only person who":* James Hollis, *Finding Meaning in the Second Half of Life* (New York: Gotham Books, 2005).

37   *"Everyone is screwed up":* Anne Lamott, *Small Victories: Spotting Improbable Moments of Grace* (New York: Riverhead, 2014).

38   *"The truth will set you free":* David Foster Wallace, *Infinite Jest* (Boston: Little, Brown, 1996).

3 TYPE EIGHT: THE CHALLENGER

56   *Eights always want to know who has the power:* Helen Palmer, *The Enneagram: Exploring the Nine Psychological Types and Their Inter-Relationships in Love and Life* (Sounds True Audio Learning Course, 2005), 8 CDs or audio download, www.soundstrue.com/store/the-enneagram-3534.html.

59   *Father Ronald Rolheiser describes* eros: Ronald Rolheiser, *The Holy Longing: The Search for a Christian Spirituality* (New York: Doubleday, 1999).

61   *"Embracing our vulnerabilities":* Brené Brown, *The Gifts of Imperfection: Let Go of Who You Think You're Supposed to Be and Embrace Who You Are* (Center City, MN: Hazelden, 2010).

4 TYPE NINE: THE PEACEMAKER

65   *"sweethearts of the Enneagram":* Susan Reynolds, *The Everything Enneagram Book: Identify Your Type, Gain Insight into Your Personality, and Find Success in Life, Love, and Business* (Avon, MA: F+W Media, 2010).

66   *"one wild and precious life":* Mary Oliver, *New and Selected Poems* (Boston: Beacon Press, 1992).

68   *"Further up and further in!"* C. S. Lewis, *The Last Battle* (New York: HarperCollins, 2001).

69   *Nines can embody the idealism of Ones:* Don Richard Riso and Russ Hudson, *The Wisdom of the Enneagram: The Complete Guide to Psychological and Spiritual Growth for the Nine Personality Types* (New York: Bantam, 1999).

69   *"The only type the Nine is not like":* Ibid.

69-71   This section draws from Eli Jaxon-Bear, *From Fixation to Freedom: The Enneagram of Liberation* (Bolinas, CA: Leela Foundation, 2001).

70   *"Being with a Nine":* Lynette Sheppard, *The Everyday Enneagram: A Personality Map for Enhancing Your Work, Love, and Life—Every Day* (Petaluma, CA: Nine Points, 2000).

75   *Bill Clinton and Newt Gingrich story:* American Experience, *Clinton,* 2012, Program Transcript, www.pbs.org/wgbh/americanexperience/features/transcript/clinton-transcript.

80   *When a Nine gets sidetracked:* Jaxon-Bear, *From Fixation to Freedom.*

5 TYPE ONE: THE PERFECTIONIST

92   *"Before I can live with other folks":* Harper Lee, *To Kill a Mockingbird* (Franklin Center, PA: Franklin Library, 1977).

92   *"Miss Jean Louise?":* Ibid.

92   *"With him, life was routine":* Ibid.

94   *"good in the worst sense of the word":* commonly attributed to Mark Twain.

102   *"20-ton shield":* Brené Brown, *The Gifts of Imperfection: Let Go of Who You Think You're Supposed to Be and Embrace Who You Are* (Center City, MN: Hazelden, 2010).

108   *"You're imperfect, and you're wired for struggle":* Brené Brown, "The Power of Vulnerability," TEDxHouston, June 2010, www.ted.com/talks/brene_brown_on_vulnerability?language=en.

6 TYPE TWO: THE HELPER

127   *If Twos are going to learn how to attend to their own needs:* Helen Palmer, *The Enneagram: Exploring the Nine Psychological Types and Their Inter-Relationships in Love and Life* (Sounds True Audio Learning Course, 2005), 8 CDs or audio download, www.soundstrue.com/store/the-enneagram-3534.html.

7 TYPE THREE: THE PERFORMER

133   *"No man, for any considerable period":* Nathaniel Hawthorne, *The Scarlet Letter* (New York: Bloom's Literary Criticism, 2007).

135   *sometimes Threes will pretend to be interested:* Kathleen V. Hurley and Theodore Elliott Dobson, *What's My Type? Use the Enneagram System of Nine Personality Types to Discover Your Best Self* (San Francisco: HarperSanFrancisco, 1991).

138   *"tell the difference between loving me and loving tennis":* Andre Agassi, *Open: An Autobiography* (New York: Vintage Books, 2010).

140   *a "Three's heart is in their work":* Helen Palmer, *The Enneagram in Love and Work: Understanding Your Intimate and Business Relationships* (San Francisco: HarperSanFrancisco, 1995).

141   *the saddest number on the Enneagram is an unsuccessful Three:* Richard Rohr and Andreas Ebert, *The Enneagram: A Christian Perspective* (New York: Crossroad, 2001).

8 TYPE FOUR: THE ROMANTIC

152   *"ruled by a hidden shame":* Richard Rohr and Andreas Ebert, *The Enneagram: A Christian Perspective* (New York: Crossroad, 2001).

153   *"irredeemable deficiency":* Beatrice M. Chestnut, *The Complete Enneagram: 27 Paths to Greater Self-Knowledge* (Berkeley, CA: She Writes, 2013).

156   *"the sense of alienation, their conscious search for identity":* Tom Condon, "The Nine Enneagram Styles: Type Fours," Center for Spiritual Resources website, www.thecsr.org/resource-directory/the-nine-enneagram-styles-type-fours.

160   *a push-pull dance:* Helen Palmer, *The Enneagram: Understanding Yourself and the Others in Your Life* (San Francisco: HarperSanFrancisco, 1991).

161   *"detach without withdrawing":* Ibid.

163   *avoid saying things to them like, "Why can't you write copy like Andrew does?":* Ibid.

9 TYPE FIVE: THE INVESTIGATOR

183   *If they're high enough on the corporate ladder:* Helen Palmer, *The Enneagram: Exploring the Nine Psychological Types and Their Inter-Relationships in Love and Life* (Sounds True Audio Learning Course, 2005), 8 CDs or audio download, www.soundstrue.com/store/the-enneagram-3534.html.

185   *"The ultimate goal of detachment":* David G. Benner, "Detachment and Engagement," Dr. David G. Benner (website and blog), September 22, 2012, www.drdavidgbenner.ca/detachment-and-engagement.

10 TYPE SIX: THE LOYALIST

192   *"If everything seems to be going well":* Steven Wright, Good Reads quotes, www.goodreads.com/quotes/77987-if-everything-seems-to-be-going-well-you-have-obviously.

196   *Six kids pick up small cues:* Beatrice M. Chestnut, *The Complete Enneagram: 27 Paths to Greater Self-Knowledge* (Berkeley, CA: She Writes, 2013).

200   *Sixes have an odd tendency:* Helen Palmer, *The Enneagram: Exploring the Nine Psychological Types and Their Inter-Relationships in Love and Life* (Sounds True Audio Learning Course, 2005), 8 CDs or audio download, www.soundstrue.com/store/the-enneagram-3534.html.

204   *"All shall be well, and all shall be well":* Julian of Norwich, *Revelations of Divine Love*, ed. Grace Warrack (London: Methuen, 1901).

11 TYPE SEVEN: THE ENTHUSIAST

209   *"scrawny necks, small mouths":* Gabor Maté, *In the Realm of Hungry Ghosts: Close Encounters with Addiction* (Berkeley, CA: North Atlantic Books, 2010).

210   *"Sevens try to imagine a life where there is no Good Friday":* Richard Rohr and Andreas Ebert, *The Enneagram: A Christian Perspective* (New York: Crossroad, 2001).

210   *"I Whistle a Happy Tune":* Richard Rodgers and Oscar Hammerstein, *The King and I*, 1951.

215   *the Epicures:* Helen Palmer, *The Enneagram: Exploring the Nine Psychological Types and Their Inter-Relationships in Love and Life* (Sounds True Audio Learning Course, 2005), 8 CDs or audio download, www.soundstrue.com/store/the-enneagram-3534.html.

218   *because they treasure their independence:* Ibid.

224   *"He who fears he shall suffer":* Michel de Montaigne, *The Complete Essays*, trans. and ed. M. A. Screech (New York: Penguin, 1993).

224   *"In a world of tension":* Thomas Merton, *Cistercian Life* (1974; repr., Our Lady of Holy Spirit Abbey, 2001).

12 SO NOW WHAT? THE BEGINNING OF LOVE

227   *"When our hearts are small, our understanding and compassion are limited":* Thich Nhat Hanh, *How to Love* (Berkeley, CA: Parallax Press, 2015).

230   *"For me to be a saint":* Thomas Merton, *New Seeds of Contemplation* (1961; repr., New York: New Directions, 2007), 31.

230   *May you recognize:* John O'Donohue, "For Solitude," in *To Bless the Space Between Us: A Book of Blessings* (New York: Doubleday, 2008).

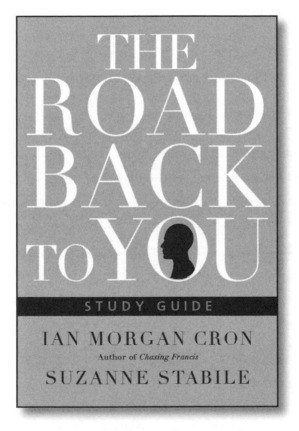

The Road Back to You Study Guide
978-0-8308-4620-7

formatio

TRADITION. EXPERIENCE.
TRANSFORMATION.

Formatio books from InterVarsity Press follow the rich tradition of the church in the journey of spiritual formation. These books are not merely about being informed, but about being transformed by Christ and conformed to his image. Formatio stands in InterVarsity Press's evangelical publishing tradition by integrating God's Word with spiritual practice and by prompting readers to move from inward change to outward witness. InterVarsity Press uses the chambered nautilus for Formatio, a symbol of spiritual formation because of its continual spiral journey outward as it moves from its center. We believe that each of us is made with a deep desire to be in God's presence. Formatio books help us to fulfill our deepest desires and to become our true selves in light of God's grace.